Oxford International Primary History

6

Peter Rebman

Oxford International Primary for enquiring minds

OXFORD

Great Clarendon Street, Oxford, OX2 6DP, United Kingdom

Oxford University Press is a department of the University of Oxford. It furthers the University's objective of excellence in research, scholarship, and education by publishing worldwide. Oxford is a registered trade mark of Oxford University Press in the UK and in certain other countries.

The moral rights of the author have been asserted.

First published in 2017

British Library Cataloguing in Publication Data
Data available

ISBN 978-0-19-841814-6

3 5 7 9 10 8 6 4 2

Paper used in the production of this book is a natural, recyclable product made from wood grown in sustainable forests. The manufacturing process conforms to the environmental regulations of the country of origin.

Printed in India by Replika Press Pvt. Ltd

Acknowledgements

Cover illustration: Carlos Molinari/Advocate Arti

Artwork: Aptara

Photos: p4/5: The Sea Warriors (gouache on paper), English School, (20th century)/Private Collection/© Look and Learn/Bridgeman Images; **p5:** Gjermundbu Viking Helmet (metallic), Viking, (10th century)/Universitetets Oldsaksamlingen, University of Oslo, Norway/Photo © AISA/Bridgeman Images; **p5, p21, p37:** ensiferum/Shutterstock; **p5, p21, p37:** Jane Rix/Shutterstock; **p7:** A Viking raid, Nicolle, Pat (Patrick) (1907-95)/Private Collection/© Look and Learn/Bridgeman Images; **p10 (T):** Werner Forman/Getty; **p10 (B):** Werner Forman/Getty; **p14:** robertharding/Alamy; **p16:** Annular brooch, Ardagh Hoard, Reerasta, County Limerick, Viking Age (silver-gilt), Celtic, (9th century)/National Museum of Ireland, Dublin, Ireland/Photo © Boltin Picture Library/Bridgeman Images; **p17 (T):** Heritage Image Partnership Ltd/Alamy; **p17 (B):** akg-images; **p20/21:** The 'Pinta', the 'Nina' and the 'Santa Maria' sailing towards the West Indies in 1492, from The Discovery of America, 1878 (colour litho), Spanish School, (19th century)/Private Collection/Index/Bridgeman Images; **p21:** World map by Martellus, including the Cape of Good Hope, rounded by Bartolomé Dias in 1488/British Library, London, UK/© British Library Board. All Rights Reserved/Bridgeman Images; **p23 (L) & p68 (L):** The only complete example of a spherical astrolabe/Werner Forman Archive/Bridgeman Images; **p23 (R):** Turkey/Middle East: Arab astronomers use an astrolabe and a cross-staff to try to determine latitude in an observatory in Constantinople./Pictures from History/Bridgeman Images; **p25 (L) & p68 (R):** Culture Club/Getty; **p25 (R):** The Academy of Baccio Bandinelli, 1547 (etching), Vico, Enea (1523-1567)/Gabinetto dei Disegni e Stampe, Galleria Degli Uffizi, Florence, Italy/Bridgeman Images; **p26:** Universal History Archive/Getty; **p29:** Columbus at the Royal Court of Spain in Barcelona (colour litho), Searles, Victor A. (fl.1892)/Private Collection/Bridgeman Images; **p32:** The Development of Printing, plate 5 from 'Nova Reperta' (New Discoveries) engraved by Philip Galle (1537-1612) c.1600 (engraving), Straet, Jan van der (Giovanni Stradano) (1523-1605) (after)/Private Collection/Bridgeman Images; **p36/37:** Kiev.Victor/Shutterstock; **p36:** Queen Elizabeth I, 'The Ermine Portrait', 1585 (oil on panel), Hilliard, Nicholas (1547-1619) / Hatfield House, Hertfordshire, UK / Bridgeman Images; **p40:** ullstein bild/Getty; **p41 (L):** architecture UK/Alamy; **p41 (R):** Man Ploughing a Field (woodcut) (b/w photo), English School, (16th century)/Private Collection/Bridgeman Images; **p44 (L):** Art Directors & TRIP/Alamy; **p44 (R):** Illustrations of Ancient Games: Football (engraving), English School, (19th century)/Private Collection/© Look and Learn/Peter Jackson Collection/Bridgeman Images; **p45:** Lordprice Collection/Alamy; **p48 (T):** Archivart/Alamy; **p48 (B):** Queen Elizabeth I - The Pelican Portrait, c.1574 (oil on panel), Hilliard, Nicholas (1547-1619)/Walker Art Gallery, National Museums Liverpool/Bridgeman Images; **p49:** Classic Image/Alamy; **p51 (L):** World History Archive/Alamy; **p51 (R):** ACTIVE MUSEUM/Alamy; **p52/53:** Arcaid Images/Alamy; **p54 & p66:** © Look and Learn; **p55:** Geography Photos/Getty; **p56:** Justin Kase zsixz/Alamy; **p57:** Heritage Images/Getty; **p59 & p67 (B):** © Look and Learn; **p60 (T):** Print Collector/Getty; **p60 (B):** ©Antiquarian Images/Mary Evans; **p61 & p69 (L):** John McKenna/Alamy; **p63 (L):** Hulton Archive/Getty; **p63 (R):** Mary Evans Picture Library; **p64:** William Vandivert/Getty; **p65 (L), p67 (T) & p69 (M):** Everett Historical/Shutterstock; **p65 (R) & p69 (R):** Marek Stepan/Alamy;

Although we have made every effort to trace and contact all copyright holders before publication this has not been possible in all cases. If notified, the publisher will rectify any errors or omissions at the earliest opportunity.

Contents

1 The Vikings

In this unit you will:

- explain who the Vikings were
- recall how, why and where the Vikings travelled
- describe how the Vikings were ruled
- recall what life was like in a Viking village
- describe the achievements that the Vikings are known for

The Vikings came from an area of northern Europe called Scandinavia, which includes Norway, Sweden and Denmark. More than 1000 years ago, the Vikings began to explore and raid countries across the world. They were fierce warriors and excellent sailors. In some places they chose to settle and build villages and farms. In other places they attacked peaceful villages and took treasure back to their homeland.

navigator
warrior   craftsperson
merchant

? Look at the images on these two pages. Based on these images, write what you think the Vikings were like.

A Viking helmet

The Vikings
c700 CE–1100 CE

The Age of Discovery and Exploration
c1400 CE–1600 CE

The Tudors
1485 CE–1603 CE

700 CE

1600 CE

The Vikings of northern Europe were at their most powerful from 700 to 1100 CE. The Vikings were also known as Norsemen, which means 'people from the North'. The Vikings are famous for being fierce warriors and great explorers. Who, exactly, were the Vikings? Where did the Vikings raid and explore? Why did the Vikings raid and explore so many countries?

The Vikings

The Vikings were from the countries of Norway, Denmark and Sweden. Collectively, these three countries are known as Scandinavia. The Scandinavian countries contain many rivers and lakes and are bordered by seas. Surrounded by all this water, the Vikings became excellent boat builders and **navigators**, which means people who explore by sea.

Why did the Vikings start exploring the world?

By the end of the 8th century CE, the Vikings were looking for new places to live. Scandinavia was becoming very overcrowded. There was not enough good farmland for everyone to have their own farm. Also, the eldest son usually inherited all of his father's land, so younger sons had to leave home to find wealth. The younger sons travelled to other countries to start new farms or to steal treasure.

Raiding, trading and exploring

The Vikings travelled long distances in their boats. Some of their voyages were violent raids. Gangs of Vikings attacked towns and villages near the coast or next to rivers. They stole anything of value they could find such as gold, jewels, books, food, cattle, clothes and tools.

This map shows the areas of Viking settlements and raids from the 8th to the 11th centuries CE.

Glossary words

century

goods

inherit

raid

settle

settlement

The Vikings made frequent raids by boat across Europe and beyond, even going as far as the Mediterranean Sea to raid Sicily and southern Italy. The Vikings regularly attacked southern France and the coast of Britain.

A Viking raid: the Vikings will take the stolen treasure back to their homes in Scandinavia.

The Vikings were not just fierce **warriors**. They were also skilled fishermen, farmers and **craftspeople**. They made beautiful jewellery, furniture and metalwork. Viking women were skilful weavers who produced fine, warm, patterned cloth. Viking **merchants** travelled through Europe and the Middle East trading the goods they made.

The Vikings were also great explorers. They set up villages and farms in places such as Britain and France. Viking explorers started new settlements in Iceland, Greenland and Russia. Viking explorers were the first Europeans to reach North America, in about 1000 CE. Travelling to North America was an amazing achievement – it was nearly 500 years before Europeans reached this continent again.

Activities

1 Use the information on these two pages to answer these questions.

   a Where did the Vikings come from?

   b Why were the Vikings such skilled boat builders and navigators?

   c Why did some Vikings decide to raid and settle in other countries?

2 Write a description of what is happening in the picture on this page. Make a list of the things you think the Vikings are stealing.

3 Create a timeline that shows when and where the Vikings raided and settled from the 8th to the 11th centuries. Use the map on page 6 and an atlas to help you name the areas and countries.

Challenge

Find out about the Vikings who reached North America. When did they do this? Where did they land? Did they settle for long? Did they fight with North American tribes?

Did you know?

Viking women travelled on the boats and went to war, but they did not fight. Instead, they looked after wounded soldiers and cooked for the warriors.

FINISH

The Vikings did not spend all of their time exploring and raiding new lands. In their homelands of Norway, Sweden and Denmark, the Vikings lived in small towns and villages. They farmed, fished and hunted. How were the towns and villages controlled? How was Viking society organised? Who ruled the Vikings?

Viking leaders

In early Viking times, each town or village had its own leader, called a chief. The chief controlled a large area of land. Each chief had an army of men from his town or village. Sometimes the army of a chief fought with the army of another local chief to gain more land. Over time, some chiefs became more and more rich and powerful as they gained more land and controlled more people. By 1000 CE, each of the Viking countries, Sweden, Norway and Denmark, had just one king who ruled the whole county.

Tough kings

When a Viking king died, all his sons had an equal right to inherit his land. This sometimes led to fierce fighting between royal families. For example, in 930 CE, King Eric of Norway killed two of his brothers so he could rule. A few years later, Eric's younger brother, Haakon, fought against Eric. Eric escaped from Norway and settled in Britain. Haakon then became King of Norway and ruled from 934 to 961 CE.

Viking society

Under the king, Viking society had three social classes: the jarls, the karls and the thralls.

Jarls were the richest and most powerful local chiefs. They owned lots of land and lived in the largest houses. They employed other Vikings to work for them. The jarls also kept slaves. Sometimes a jarl became very powerful and challenged the king for the throne.

Karls belonged to the middle class. This group included farmers, merchants and craftspeople. This was the group that traded with other countries and went to war and on raids.

Thralls were the slaves. Slaves were captured in war or purchased by traders and sold in the market. If slaves ran away, they could be killed. Female thralls cooked, wove cloth and sometimes helped on the farms. Male thralls worked hard doing any work that their owner wanted them to do.

Glossary words

outlaw	society
social class	trade

They worked in the fields or mended houses, weapons and equipment. Sometimes a thrall was paid to do a skilled job. If thralls saved enough money, they could buy their way out of slavery and become free.

What about the women?

Women were not equal to men, but they had many rights that woman in other ancient cultures did not have. A woman's parents usually

chose her husband, but Viking women could own property, run businesses, inherit land and divorce their husbands. Most married women looked after the house and children. When the men travelled abroad raiding, the women were in charge of the farm too.

Viking children

Children did not go to school. They helped their parents with cooking and weaving at home or with farm work. By the time they were 15 or 16 years old, they were classed as adults.

The Thing

Each local chief had a council of karls to help him. The council met regularly at an open-air meeting called a Thing. They discussed problems, voted on new laws, settled arguments and decided on the punishment for a person who was found guilty of breaking the law.

At a Thing, accused people could defend themselves and present their side of the argument. Punishments for a criminal included being fined, outlawed or made into a slave. Rich people had to pay bigger fines. In some cases, criminals were executed.

Did you know?

Viking children usually had a patronym (a name based on their father's name) as well as their first name. For example: Leif, son of Erik, was called Leif Erikson; Freydis, daughter of Erik, was called Freydis Eriksdottir.

Activities

1   Draw a diagram to show how Viking society was organised. Show the various groups and explain the differences between them.

2   Use the information on these two pages and further research to find out more about the Thing and how criminals were punished in Viking society.

Challenge

Some Viking rulers had strange or violent names, for example Eric Bloodaxe, Sweyn Forkbeard, Bjorn Ironside and Thorfinn Skull-splitter. Find out about one Viking ruler and prepare a fact file. Include where and when he was born, when he died, what he was most famous for and any interesting facts about him.

The Vikings relied on farming, fishing and hunting for their food. Viking traders travelled far and wide selling some of the food and other goods from farming and hunting. What did the Vikings farm, fish and hunt? How important was trade? Where did Viking merchants travel to?

Farming

Viking farmers grew most of their food. They grew oats, barley and wheat to make flour and porridge. They ate vegetables such as carrots, onions, beans and cabbages – vegetables that grew well in cool climates. They kept farm animals, including sheep, goats, cattle and chickens. In autumn, farmers killed some animals to provide enough food to feed their families through the winter. However, much of the farmland in Scandinavia was poor and, as the land became more overcrowded, some Vikings decided to move to faraway lands in search of fertile soil and bigger farms.

Fishing and hunting

Many Vikings built their settlements near to the coast or rivers. Fishermen used nets to catch sea fish such as cod and herring or river fish such as salmon and trout. They caught seabirds to eat and took eggs from the nests.

The Vikings hunted wild animals such as seals, deer, foxes, wolves and bears. They ate the meat and used the fur to make warm clothes or to trade for other goods.

Before they had coins, Viking traders often bought and sold using pieces of silver. They carried a set of folding scales, which they used to weigh the silver to make sure they got a fair deal. The Vikings started to use coins during the later Viking age.

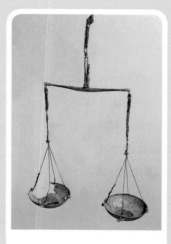

A set of Viking scales

Viking merchants

Viking merchants travelled thousands of miles buying and selling a wide range of goods. They took honey, wool, timber, iron, weapons and fur from Scandinavia to sell or trade. They also took dried fish, whale bones and walrus ivory. One of the biggest exports was amber, a yellow-orange precious stone. Some Viking traders travelled by sea to Britain or Iceland.

Amber was an important trade item for the Vikings. This amber figure was part of a Viking's chess set.

Glossary words

archeologist	founded	pottery
fertile	knarr boat	trade route

Other traders travelled over land through Russia, reaching as far south as Constantinople (which is now Istanbul in modern-day Turkey). Some merchants travelled further east to Baghdad in modern-day Iraq.

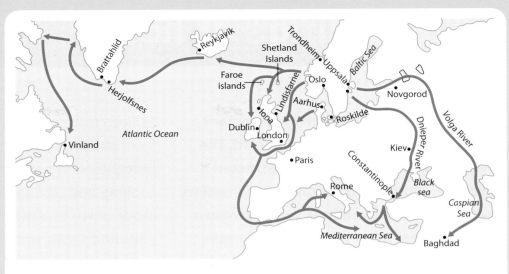

This map shows the main trade routes that Viking traders used.

The Viking merchants returned home with wheat, woollen cloth and silver from Britain, and pottery and glass from France and Germany. They traded for jewellery in Russia and spices and silks in the Middle East. Everywhere they went, the Vikings bought and sold slaves.

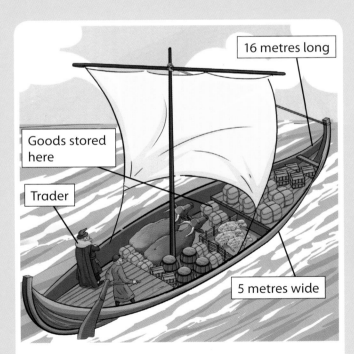

Viking traders used knarr boats. These boats were much wider than the boats used by Viking raiders, and had a pit in the middle to hold the goods safely.

Activities

1   Why do you think so many Viking settlements were built near to the coast or rivers?

2   Prepare a lesson for younger students that explains Viking farming, fishing, hunting and trade. Use presentation software and start with an image that shows what you will teach in the lesson. Try to use a map in your lesson.

Challenge

The city of Novgorod, the capital city of the first Russian state, was founded by Vikings. Find out about Novgorod. When was the city founded? Who ruled the city? What did the Vikings do there? How did Novgorod develop over time?

1.4 The Vikings at home

The Vikings lived in a tough environment. The winters were long, dark and cold. The Vikings needed warm, well-constructed buildings to protect their animals as well as the people. What buildings were there in a Viking village? How did the Vikings make their houses? What did the houses look like?

Viking towns and villages

Most Vikings lived in small villages surrounded by farms. Others lived in busy trading towns on the coast. The harbour was an important place in a Viking town. The harbour was very busy as boats were loaded and unloaded with goods and animals.

Skilled craftspeople made items to sell at the local market. Jewellers made rings and brooches, and potters made clay pots for cooking and storing food. Wood-workers made bowls and plates, leather-workers made belts and shoes, and blacksmiths made swords, spears and axes.

A Viking home

In most parts of Scandinavia, people lived in houses made of wood. The houses were usually rectangular and very long.

A There were no windows because windows would let in the cold. The houses were dark inside, lit only by oil lamps or candles.

B A smoke hole in the roof let out smoke from the fire below.

C There was space to keep some animals inside in winter.

D Food was stored in baskets.

E Homes did not have much furniture. There were only simple tables, benches and chests. People slept under blankets and furs on platforms around the edges of the room. Only rich people could afford a wooden bed.

F The Vikings ate two meals a day. They ate bread, butter and cheese in the morning. They ate the main meal after sunset. The main meal included meat or fish and vegetables. Meals were served on wooden plates or in stone bowls.

G Vikings kept a fire burning all day. They grilled food over the fire or baked food in a hole in the ground next to the fire. They cooked meat and vegetables in a pot that hung over the fire.

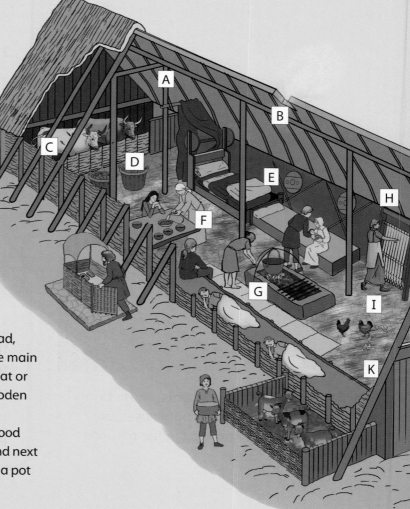

The Vikings covered the roofs of their houses with turf to help keep out the freezing cold winds. In places where there were few trees, families used stone to build their homes instead of wood.

The whole family – children, parents, grandparents, aunts, uncles and cousins – lived in the same house. Look at the picture of a Viking house. The artist has cut away part of the roof so you can see inside.

Glossary words

preserve   **turf**

H   People in the house were always busy: cooking, weaving, salting food and repairing tools and weapons.

I   There were no carpets. Rushes on the floor and animal skins on the walls helped to keep the house warm.

J   Clothes and blankets were stored in chests.

K   Most houses had just one room for everyone to share. Richer Vikings had more rooms: a small entrance hall, a large main room, bedrooms and a store room.

Activities

1   Imagine you are an estate agent in Viking times. Design a brochure or advert to sell the home shown here. Before you start, discuss with a friend all the things that are included in an estate agent's brochure. What features of the home will you focus on? What images will you include? What parts of the home do you not want to highlight?

2   In a group, write and perform a role play. Two of you are estate agents, showing buyers around a Viking home. The other students are buyers. The buyers should ask questions to test the estate agents' knowledge.

Did you know?

Salt was important for the Vikings. They bought salt from travelling merchants and used it to preserve fish and meat. In the long winter they ate the preserved food, when fresh food was scarce.

Challenge

Compare a Viking home with another home you have studied. What are the main similarities and differences between the two homes?

Be a good historian

Good historians understand how we know about people's lives in the past. The Vikings did not write their history down. However, we know a lot about what the Vikings ate based on the crops that still grow in Scandinavia today and because archeologists have found seeds and fish bones in Viking graves.

The Vikings were skilled sailors. They travelled all over Europe and beyond looking for opportunities to trade and for new lands to settle in. How far did the Vikings go? How did the Vikings travel? How did they find their way?

Viking boats

The Vikings were expert boat builders. They made fast boats from long planks of wood held in place by wooden pegs and iron nails. They overlapped the wooden planks to make the boat strong. They coated the boat with tar from pine trees to make it waterproof.

There was often a carved, wooden figurehead, such as a dragon.

Viking boats could sail at about 18 kilometres per hour.

The mast was about 12 metres high with a square sail.

Each boat held up to 40 men.

Vikings attached shields to the sides for defence.

These holes are for oars.

A longboat was 20–25 metres long.

A Viking longboat found in Oseberg, Norway

793 CE	844 CE	845 CE	860 CE	862 CE	865 CE	874 CE
Vikings raided Britain for the first time.	Vikings raided Spain.	Vikings sailed up rivers in Europe and attacked Paris, in France, and Hamburg, in Germany.	Vikings attacked Constantinople (now Istanbul), the largest and wealthiest city in Europe.	Vikings travelled along trade routes and settled in Russia.	Vikings began to settle in Britain, instead of just raiding the coast. Over the next 15 years they gradually took control of more of Britain.	Vikings settled in Iceland.

The boats, known as longboats, could be used in both deep and shallow water, making them perfect for travelling over the ocean and sailing up rivers.

How did the Vikings find their way?

The Vikings had no special instruments to guide them so they sailed close to the coast whenever possible. They looked for well-known landmarks. They also used the Sun and stars to guide them. The Vikings had good knowledge of wind and wave patterns to help them work out which direction to take. They passed on information about navigation from one generation to the next.

Viking sailors sometimes took ravens with them to help them navigate. The sailors let a raven go and watched it fly up high into the sky. If the bird saw land, it flew in that direction. The Vikings then sailed in the same direction. If the bird could not see any land, it came back down to the boat and the sailors knew they had further to travel.

How far did the Vikings travel?

The Vikings travelled far and wide as they traded, raided and settled. Look at the timeline at the bottom of the page to see where and when they travelled.

Activities

1 Write about how Viking sailors navigated at sea.

2 Work in a group to prepare an oral or digital presentation showing when and where the Vikings raided, traded and explored. Include a map in your presentation.

Did you know?

Boats were so important to the Vikings that some kings were buried in boats with all their treasures.

Challenge

Write a short biography of one of these famous Viking explorers: Bjarni Herjólfsson, Leif Erikson, Erik the Red or Ingólfur Arnarson.

900 CE
Vikings raided coasts all around the Mediterranean Sea. In Britain, Vikings ruled the north of Scotland, parts of Ireland and the east and north of England.

911 CE
Vikings settled in northern France. The area they settled in is called Normandy after the Viking settlers from the north.

983 CE
Vikings, led by 'Erik the Red', settled in Greenland.

986 CE
A Viking, named Bjarni Herjólfsson, was blown off course in a storm. He briefly landed in Canada.

1001 CE
A settler from Greenland, Leif Erikson, landed in places he named Helluland, Markland and Vinland. Today, we know that these places are on the east coast of North America.

The name Viking means 'pirate' or 'raider' in Old Norse (the Viking language). The Vikings were feared by the people they attacked. However, the Vikings were not just fierce warriors. Viking merchants travelled to other countries to trade, not raid. They also went looking for new places to live. What other achievements are the Vikings known for?

Viking craftspeople

The Vikings were highly skilled craftspeople and made most of the things they needed, such as their strong, fast boats. They made many other items to sell or trade. The Vikings used leather to make shoes, belts and clothing. Viking carpenters made beautifully carved furniture and toys and they knew how to cut wood to give it maximum strength.

Loom

The material was coloured with dyes made from plants and rocks.

Weights to keep the threads straight and tight

In Viking homes, women wove linen (from a plant called flax) or wool into cloth on a loom.

Metal-workers made tools, locks, armour, axes and swords. They travelled from farm to farm to mend broken tools.

Viking jewellery

Both Viking men and women loved to wear jewellery. They wore rings, bracelets and necklaces. Poorer Vikings owned jewellery made from bone, jet (a hard, black stone) or bronze. Richer Vikings owned jewellery made from silver and gold. The Vikings did not have buttons or zips, so they used belts, pins and brooches to keep their clothes in place.

A Viking brooch, made from silver and amber

Games, music and sport

The Vikings liked to enjoy themselves. They enjoyed swimming, fishing and boating. In the winter, they skated on ice and skied on the snow. The Vikings played chess and used dice. Many of the sports they played were good training for war, for example spear-throwing, wrestling and archery.

The Vikings had three big festivals a year – at the start of summer, at harvest time and in the winter. The festivals continued for many days. A festival was a time for eating, drinking and relaxing. There were acrobats, jugglers and poets. People played traditional music, danced and told stories. The Vikings were great storytellers. Their stories of exciting adventures and heroes are known as sagas. The Vikings passed on these stories from one generation to the next.

Could the Vikings read and write?

Reading and writing were not common among the Vikings. The Vikings who could read and write did not use paper and pens. Instead, they used metal tools to cut letters and pictures into stone, wood and bone. The Vikings had a basic alphabet that they used to tell stories, record events, send messages and label valuable items. The Vikings left few written records or pictures. Instead, parents told stories to their children, who told them to their children.

A Viking picture stone with letters around the edge. This picture stone was found in Sweden and dates from the 11th century CE.

Did you know?

Viking merchants watched people playing chess in the Middle East. When they returned home, the merchants brought chess boards and pieces with them. Chess became very popular among the Vikings.

These Viking chess pieces were discovered in Scotland in 1831. They are carved from walrus ivory and whales' teeth.

Glossary words

armour	festival	record
event	linen	saga

Activities

1 Design a poster or write a short report on the achievements of the Vikings. Find images of Viking jewellery, crafts, games and writing to illustrate your poster or report.

2 Why are the Vikings best known for attacking other countries rather than for any of their other achievements? Write down all the reasons you can think of.

Challenge

Research the Viking alphabet and write a short report. How many letters were there? What were the letters called?

① Review

Answer these questions in your notebook.

Choose the best answer from the choices below. Write a, b or c as your answer.

1   The Vikings originally came from Scandinavia. Which are the three countries in Scandinavia?
   a   Norway, Sweden and Spain
   b   Norway, Denmark and Sweden
   c   Denmark, Sweden and Britain

2   The Vikings were also known as:
   a   Norsemen
   b   Eastmen
   c   Westmen

3   The richest and most powerful Viking chiefs were called:
   a   jarls
   b   karls
   c   thralls

4   Groups of Vikings had regular open-air meetings to discuss local problems, vote on new laws and settle arguments. A meeting like this was called a:
   a   Thing
   b   Thrall
   c   King

5   The long, wide boat used by Viking traders was called a:
   a   knarr
   b   canoe
   c   coracle

6   The metal that Viking merchants used when trading for goods was:
   a   gold
   b   iron
   c   silver

7   How many meals did the Vikings eat per day?
   a   one
   b   two
   c   three

8   In 986 CE, a Viking explorer landed in Canada and was the first European to reach North America. His name was:
   a   Erik the Red
   b   Bjarni Herjólfsson
   c   Leif Erikson

9   Vikings raided Britain for the first time in:
   a   793 CE
   b   893 CE
   c   993 CE

10 The Vikings were great storytellers. The stories they told were called:
    a togas
    b sagas
    c chronicles

Decide if these statements are true or false. Write 'True' or 'False' for each one.

11 The name Viking means 'merchant' or 'trader'.
12 The Vikings wrote about kings, battles and other important events on paper and in books.

Now complete these tasks.

13 Look at the list below. It gives some possible reasons why the Vikings chose to leave their homeland and travel to another country.

> - There were too many people in Scandinavia and there was not enough farmland for everyone.
> - Other countries had many treasures.
> - Scandinavia is rocky and covered in forest so the land was not good for farming.
> - Only the eldest son inherited the family farm. Younger sons had to go and find their own land.
> - The Vikings were strong warriors. They wanted to prove their strength by fighting others.
> - The Vikings wanted to explore and discover new places to trade with.

    a Think carefully about each reason. Make a list of reasons why a farmer might choose to travel. Make another list of reasons why a raider might choose to travel. Sort your two lists into order from the most important reason to the least important reason.

    b When you have prepared your lists, answer the following question: Why did Vikings leave their homeland and travel to other countries?

14 Imagine that you live in a country in which the Vikings have settled. Your tribe has sent you to spy on a new settlement of Vikings to find out what these strange and fierce people are really like. Describe the Vikings' homes, villages and towns. Describe the Viking people.

15 Write a report about the impact of the Vikings on a country that you have not already studied. Use this book and further research to find out about:
    - when the Vikings started raiding or trading with the country
    - how the Vikings travelled to this country
    - what items the Vikings traded with this country
    - how much of the country the Vikings settled in
    - the positive and negative impacts of the Vikings on this country
    - how the Vikings have influenced modern-day life in this country.

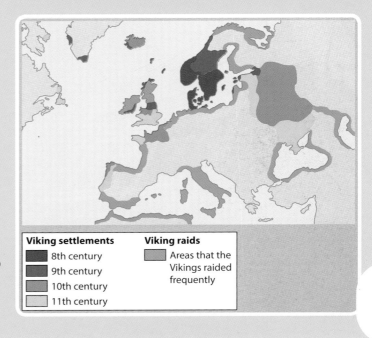

Viking settlements
8th century
9th century
10th century
11th century

Viking raids
Areas that the Vikings raided frequently

2 The Age of Discovery and Exploration

In this unit you will:

- recall what the 'Golden Age' means
- explain how trade and ideas spread before the Age of Discovery and Exploration
- analyse why there was an Age of Discovery and Exploration
- recall some of the key voyages at this time
- describe what life was like on a ship at this time

About 600 years ago, Europeans began to find out more about the world. This period is known as the Age of Discovery and Exploration. It began in the 1400s CE and continued to the 1600s CE. During this time, there were many new discoveries about science, medicine, art and culture. Many of these discoveries were made by people outside Europe. European **explorers** brought the new ideas to Europe when they returned home. This was a time when Europeans discovered new routes to India, the Far East and the Americas.

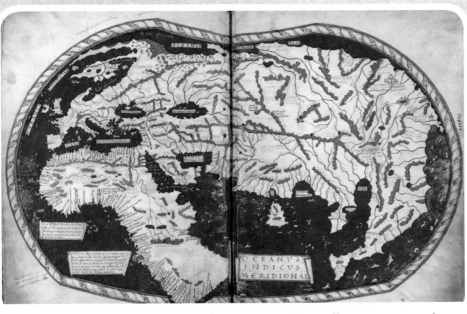

This map was made in 1489 CE by Henricus Martellus, a map-maker from Germany. The map shows what Europeans thought the world looked like at that time.

? Look at the map on this page.

1 When this map was drawn, European explorers had visited much of the west coast of Africa, but they had not explored much of the east coast. How can you tell?

2 Make a list of some of the places in the world that Europeans had not discovered in 1489 but that we know exist today. Use an atlas to help you.

> **explorer**
> **Middle Ages**
> **scholar   Renaissance**

The Vikings
c700 CE–1100 CE

The Age of Discovery and Exploration
c1400 CE–1600 CE

The Tudors
1485 CE–1603 CE

700 CE

1600 CE

In Europe, the 1400s and 1500s CE are known as a time of great discovery and exploration. European merchants found new trade routes. New ideas and inventions changed how Europeans thought about the world. How did trade and ideas spread before this time? What was the impact of the trade and ideas?

Trade and travel in the Middle East

For many hundreds of years before the 1400s and 1500s, the centre of the trading world was the Middle East. Merchants from India and the Far East travelled to Middle Eastern cities to sell silk, spices, carpets and precious jewels to European traders. The European traders brought goods from Europe, such as woollen cloth, iron, timber and salt, to sell in the Middle East, and to traders from India and the Far East. About 1000 years ago, Baghdad was a central 'trading hub' and one of the biggest cities in the world.

This is a trading list of goods traded in Baghdad in the 9th century CE.

- From China: spices, silk, porcelain, paper, ink, horses, saddles, rhubarb
- From the Byzantines: silver and gold vessels, coins, medicines, cloth, slaves, experts in water engineering and farming
- From Arabia: horses, camels, animal skins
- From North Africa: leopards and black falcons
- From Yemen: cloaks, giraffes, armour, indigo
- From Egypt: donkeys, fine cloth
- From Central Asia: slaves, armour, helmets, grapes, sugar
- From Persia: plums, soft woollen coats, honey, fruit drinks, glass

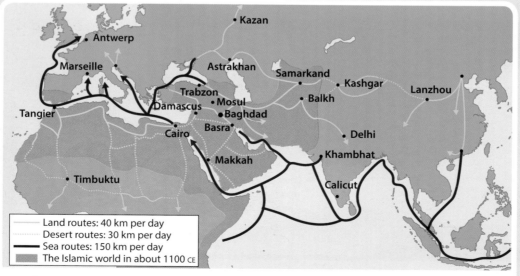

Land routes: 40 km per day
Desert routes: 30 km per day
Sea routes: 150 km per day
The Islamic world in about 1100 CE

Arab trade in the **Middle Ages**: merchants travelled by land and sea.

Glossary words

astronomy

engineering

indigo

invention

observatory

technology

A Golden Age in the Middle East

The Middle East was far ahead of many European countries in science, medicine, engineering, mathematics and astronomy. There were vast libraries and colleges in Baghdad that attracted the best students (known as **scholars**) from around the world. The scholars translated the books of writers from Ancient Greece and Ancient Rome, as well as from India, China and Persia. As a result, ancient knowledge was preserved for future generations. Over time, inventions and ideas from the Middle East spread to Europe. Here are some examples.

The astronomer al-Fazari invented an instrument called the astrolabe. The astrolabe made it possible to work out direction and location when travelling. European travellers and sailors soon began to use this new technology.

An astrolabe from 1480 CE. It is signed 'Work of Musa'.

Ibn Sina wrote a medical textbook known as the 'Canon'. The book was used for hundreds of years to train doctors in many different parts of the world.

Omar Khayyam was an Arab mathematician, astronomer, geographer and poet. He wrote rules for algebra that influenced mathematicians for hundreds of years. The word 'algebra' comes from the Arabic 'al-jabr', which means 'reunion of broken parts'.

Astronomers built large observatories for viewing the stars. The common names of over 100 stars are based on their Arabic names.

Challenge

Research the period that historians call the Golden Age of Islam. Find three examples of developments in medicine, art, biology, physics and engineering.

Activities

1   Look at the map on page 22. Explain why historians say that the Middle East was at the centre of the trading world at this time.

2   Look at the list of goods traded in Baghdad. Imagine you are a Baghdad merchant. Design a poster to advertise the goods you have for sale and to show that the goods have come from all over the world.

3   Why do you think this period was called a Golden Age in the Middle East?

In the 15th century CE, Europeans began to make new discoveries about the world. Merchants found new trade routes and explorers set out on daring and dangerous expeditions. Why did people try to find new trade routes and explore other countries? Why did people become more curious about the world around them?

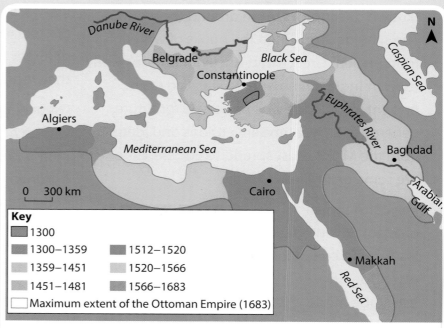

Expansion of the Ottoman Empire, 1300–1683

Key
- 1300
- 1300–1359
- 1359–1451
- 1451–1481
- 1512–1520
- 1520–1566
- 1566–1683
- Maximum extent of the Ottoman Empire (1683)

Exploration and trade

European merchants and explorers had always looked for new lands. Some explorers wanted the excitement of discovering places that no European had ever seen before. Other explorers wanted to find new trading partners and new goods to bring back and sell.

A changing world

The Age of Discovery and Exploration began in the 1400s. It was caused by some important changes in the world.

In the early 1300s, several powerful tribes began to conquer the Middle East. One tribe, the Ottomans from north-east Turkey, began building an empire. Over the next 200 years, the Ottoman Empire grew until it stretched from the Euphrates River near the Arabian Gulf to the Danube River in Hungary. As their empire grew, the Ottomans took control of many of the key trading cities in the Middle East.

The Ottomans put taxes on all goods coming into and out of their empire. This made the goods more expensive. European traders did not want to pay the high taxes, so they looked for alternative routes to travel directly to India and the Far East to buy silk, spices, carpets and precious jewels to sell in Europe. Soon, traders from two of the most powerful countries in Europe, Spain and Portugal, set out to find a new way to the East by sea. While the traders were looking for a new route, they discovered some amazing places. A new age of exploration had begun.

Glossary words

conquer	manuscript	tax
discover	scientist	tribe
empire	sculptor	

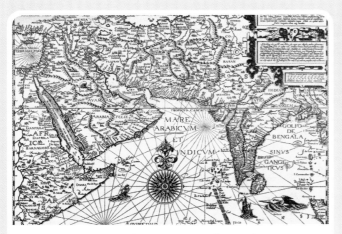

A European merchant's map from the 1500s CE. Merchants took maps like this with them when trading in the area.

A new age of learning

As the Ottomans began to take over more and more land, many scholars in the Middle East decided to move away. The people who moved were some of the world's best writers, musicians, astronomers, architects, artists, scientists and mathematicians.

The Middle Eastern scholars settled in different parts of Europe, but most of them settled in Italy. They founded schools and colleges in cities such as Florence and Padua. The Middle Eastern scholars brought with them manuscripts and books written in Ancient Greece and Rome, as well as their own knowledge.

Much of the ancient knowledge had been forgotten in Europe.

When the European scholars read about the things that had been discovered in the ancient world, they were amazed. Europeans realised that many of their own ideas were wrong. For example, in Europe, a common way of treating a mild infection of an arm or a leg was to cut off the arm or leg! However, in the Middle East people treated an infection with ointment, rest and a healthy diet.

Italy was a centre of European learning where scholars discussed new ideas and experimented with new techniques.

Soon, European sculptors, artists, doctors and scientists began to look at the world in a new way. They began to experiment and test new ideas to seek out answers. Before long, new discoveries were made in science, medicine and technology. A new age of discovery in Europe had begun.

Did you know?

The new age of discovery and learning in Europe from the 1400s to the 1600s is often called the **Renaissance**. This is a French word that means 'rebirth'.

Activities

1 Describe the growth of the Ottoman Empire. Use the map on page 24 to help you with important dates.

2 Write a few sentences to explain how the growth of the Ottoman Empire led to:

   a a new age of exploration

   b a new age of discovery.

Challenge

Use books and the Internet to research the history of Istanbul. Create a timeline showing the five most important dates in the city's history. Explain why you have chosen these dates.

2.3a Voyages of discovery and exploration

The Age of Discovery and Exploration was a time when Europeans began exploring the world by sea in search of new trade routes, new goods and new trading partners. Some explorers set sail because they wanted to explore the unknown and learn more about their world. What discoveries did the explorers make?

Portugal leads the way

After the Ottomans took control of the Middle East, North Africa and south-east Europe, they put taxes on goods passing through their land. European merchants looked for new trade routes to the East. They wanted to travel by sea to avoid having to pay tax to the Ottomans.

Portugal was a leading European nation at this time. Prince Henry, the Portuguese king's son, encouraged Portuguese sailors to find new sea routes. In 1488 CE, he founded a school of navigation, science and map-making and helped pay for voyages. In 1488 CE, Portuguese explorer Bartolomeu Dias was the first European to sail around the southern tip of Africa and into the Indian Ocean.

A modern picture of Vasco da Gama meeting an Indian prince shortly after arriving in India in 1498 CE

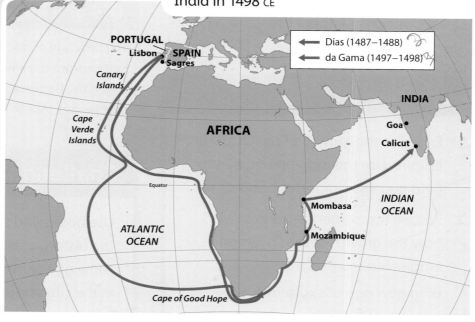

The voyages of Dias and da Gama

In 1498 CE, Vasco da Gama became the first European to sail around Africa and land in India. He returned with his ship full of goods such as silk, spices and jewels.

New technology

There were a number of developments in shipbuilding and navigation at this time. For example, better sails made ships easier to steer. Also, Europeans had started to use astrolabes (see page 23), which made it possible to work out direction and location when sailing.

Did you know?

When Vasco da Gama returned to Portugal, he sold the goods that he brought home from India for 60 times more than they cost him.

A new theory

In the late 1400s, Europeans started to believe that it was possible to reach India and China (which are to the east of Europe) by sailing west across the Atlantic Ocean. In other words, explorers and merchants hoped to sail all around the Earth by sea, instead of having to go over land, or around the bottom of Africa.

In 1492, an explorer and merchant named Christopher Columbus set out west across the Atlantic. He, like everyone else in Europe, had no idea that the continents of North and South America were in the way. What he discovered would change the way people viewed the world!

Activities

1   Use the information on these pages to explain:

   a why Columbus wanted to find a new route to India and China

   b how he hoped to find a new route to India and China.

2   Describe the contribution of Portugal to the Age of Discovery and Exploration.

Glossary words

development   voyage

Challenge

Prepare a fact file about someone who has been regarded as a 'great explorer' in the last 100 years. Who was the explorer? What did the person explore? Why is this explorer seen as 'great'?

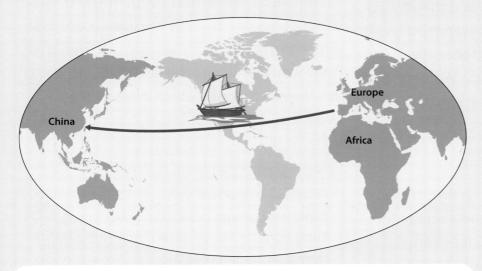

China   Europe   Africa

Columbus thought he could sail directly to China from Europe. He did not know that North and South America existed.

2.3b Voyages of discovery and exploration

Columbus prepares

Christopher Columbus hoped to reach India and China by sailing west from Europe across the Atlantic Ocean. Long-distance voyages were very expensive so Columbus tried to borrow money from the king of Portugal. The king refused to lend money for the voyage. The king felt that Portugal had already found a successful route to India so he did not need to pay for Columbus to find another. Eventually, Queen Isabella of Spain agreed to help pay for the ships and supplies that Columbus needed.

Columbus bought three ships and hired 100 sailors to help him. He set off across the Atlantic Ocean on 3 August 1492 CE.

Across the sea

The voyage went well for six weeks. The sailors in Columbus's crew were content. They occasionally went swimming, and they fished and sang together. Columbus even read books to them. However, by early October, the sailors were becoming unhappy. Water and food supplies were low and there was no sign of India or China.

Land at last

Eventually, on 12 October 1492, one of the sailors saw land. Columbus and some of the crew sailed to the shore. They reached a small island in the Caribbean Sea that Columbus named San Salvador.

Columbus also sailed to other islands in the Caribbean such as Cuba and Hispaniola. He met natives there but was disappointed not to find the busy Chinese ports he had expected. However, he was convinced he had landed on islands near to China. He soon set sail for home, taking gold, fish and parrots with him back to Spain.

A new hero

When Columbus returned home he was treated like a hero. He made three more trips to these new islands and also landed on the South American mainland. Until his death in 1506, Columbus always believed that he had discovered a new route to islands near to China or India. He called the islands the Indies. They were later renamed the West Indies and are still known by this name.

Columbus had no idea he had landed on the continents of North and South America, which Europeans did not know existed. People did not realise that Columbus had discovered a 'new world' until after he had died and explorers had found other lands in 'the Americas'.

Did you know?

Explorers brought back exotic goods that Europeans had never seen before, including tomatoes, pineapples, tobacco, turkeys and cocoa.

Christopher Columbus speaking to Queen Isabella and King Ferdinand of Spain after his return from the 'new world' in 1493. He is describing his voyage and showing them what he has brought back.

Columbus – the first of many

Columbus's success inspired other explorers. The promise of wealth, new trading partners and better ships and equipment encouraged more people to explore the world.

- John Cabot set out in 1497. He was from Italy but King Henry VII of England paid for his voyage. He tried to reach the Far East by sailing west across the Atlantic Ocean. Instead, he landed in North America.

- Amerigo Vespucci (from Italy) explored the east coast of South America from 1499 to 1504. He confirmed that the land Columbus had discovered was part of a new continent. This 'new world' was named America after Vespucci's first name.

- Ferdinand Magellan (from Portugal) spent three years, from 1519 to 1522, sailing around the world. His ships were the first to complete this journey.

Glossary words

natives   exotic

Activities

1 Look at the painting above. Imagine you travelled with Columbus and you were with him when he met the king and queen of Spain. What questions did the king and queen ask? How did Columbus respond?

2 In a group, create a presentation to explain how European explorers gradually discovered more and more about the world. Include key dates, countries and explorers. Include the reasons for exploring and discovering new lands.

Challenge

Columbus set sail from Spain on 3 August 1492. He reached San Salvador, in the Bahamas, on 12 October 1492. Find out the distance he travelled. Work out how many miles he sailed per day. Compare this to the fastest method of transport between Spain and San Salvador today.

Nearly all of the great European explorers used a type of ship known as a caravel. Explorers such as Christopher Columbus, Bartolomeu Dias and Vasco da Gama all used these ships. Why did they choose these ships? What did a caravel look like? What was life like on board a caravel?

The size of a caravel compared with the size of a modern ocean liner: a caravel weighed about the same as 30 cars (50 to 60 tonnes).

What was so special about caravels?

A caravel was between 20 and 30 metres long and weighed between 50 and 60 tonnes. It was lighter and shorter than many of the other ships that sailed long distances for trade. The short length and low weight made caravels very fast, which was important for crossing large oceans. Caravels could also sail in most directions and could cope with very rough seas and high winds.

What were conditions like on a caravel?

Between 25 and 35 men were packed on board a caravel. These ships leaked badly and were very dirty. Illness was common because of the dirty and overcrowded conditions. Many sailors also suffered with a disease called scurvy, caused by not having enough vitamin C. On some journeys over half of the sailors died.

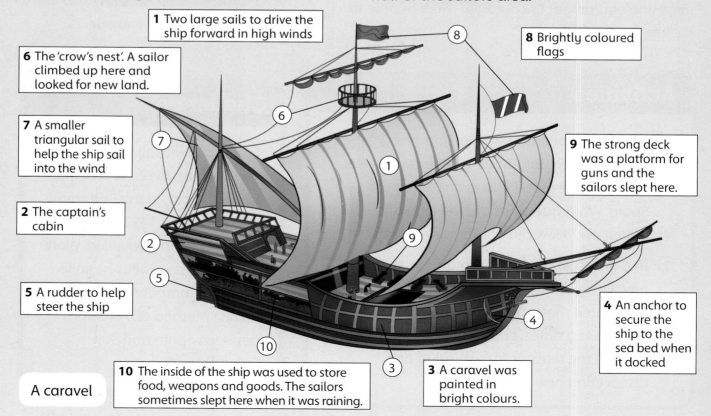

1 Two large sails to drive the ship forward in high winds

6 The 'crow's nest'. A sailor climbed up here and looked for new land.

8 Brightly coloured flags

7 A smaller triangular sail to help the ship sail into the wind

9 The strong deck was a platform for guns and the sailors slept here.

2 The captain's cabin

5 A rudder to help steer the ship

4 An anchor to secure the ship to the sea bed when it docked

10 The inside of the ship was used to store food, weapons and goods. The sailors sometimes slept here when it was raining.

3 A caravel was painted in bright colours.

A caravel

Food and water were also a problem for the sailors. The ships were at sea for many weeks and fresh food ran out quickly. When there was no fresh food left, the sailors ate salted fish and meat, dried beans and hard biscuits. Food and water were stored in barrels. The water must have tasted horrible after a few weeks at sea!

'We were three months and twenty days without fresh food. We ate old biscuits full of worms. We drank water that was yellow and stinking.'

This was written by a sailor on board one of explorer Ferdinand Magellan's ships.

The sailors had all sorts of jobs to do. They had to clean the decks, mend ropes, control the sails and pump out sea water that had come into the ship. Sailors who did not follow orders were sometimes whipped. The ship's crew was divided into groups, each of which was called a watch. The sailors in a watch worked for four hours, then had four hours to rest when the next watch took over. In bad weather, all the crew worked together.

Sailors on the explorers' ships were paid better than ordinary sailors. They also received a share of any goods or treasures they found. Some sailors went on the voyages because they loved adventure and wanted the chance to see new places.

Did you know?

In 1497, Vasco da Gama left Portugal for India with 170 men, on board 4 ships. He returned more than 2 years later with only 2 ships and 55 men. He had sailed 24 000 miles and spent 300 days at sea.

Glossary words

adventure	scurvy
caravel	watch

Activities

1 Why do you think explorers used caravels?

2 Imagine you were a sailor on board a caravel. Use all the information you have learned so far to write an account of a day at sea. Make sure you include:

   a a description of your caravel

   b conditions on board the ship

   c the problems with food and water

   d your reasons for becoming a sailor.

Challenge

One of the most famous caravels of all was called the Pinta. This was the fastest of the three ships used by Christopher Columbus on his first voyage across the Atlantic Ocean in 1492. Find out as much as you can about this ship. For example, find out the ship's length, its weight, what features made it faster than the others, who sailed on it, and other voyages it made. Find out about a sailor named Rodrigo de Triana who was on board the Pinta.

A printing press (on the right) in a printer's workshop.

This period in European history was not just a time when explorers set out in search of new lands, trade routes and wealth. It was also a time when there was an explosion of new ideas, knowledge and learning. This period was known as the Renaissance.

A 'rebirth' of learning

In the 1400s CE, the Ottomans began to take over lots of land in the Middle East. At this time, some of the best colleges and libraries in the world were in the areas that the Ottomans conquered. Many of the people working in these colleges and libraries fled to Europe. They brought their own knowledge and many ancient books and manuscripts with them.

People in Europe had never had access to this knowledge before and soon found out that the people who had lived long ago often understood the world better than they did. Across Europe, writers, sculptors, doctors, mathematicians and scientists started to realise that some of their current ideas were wrong and that there were often different ways to do things. They were inspired to try new experiments, discuss new ideas and find new ways of doing things.

Soon there were fascinating discoveries in science, medicine and engineering. This period of European discovery is known as the Renaissance, which is a French word meaning 'rebirth'. The new knowledge and ideas encouraged scholars to think in different ways.

They felt they were seeing the world clearly for the first time. They felt as if they had been reborn.

The spread of ideas

One of the most important inventions of the Renaissance period was the printing press. Many historians have compared the invention of the printing press with the invention of the Internet. Both inventions allowed ideas and information to spread far more quickly than before.

The printing press was invented in the mid-1400s. Printers used this special machine to print pages, which allowed them to produce books quickly and cheaply. Before the printing press, all books had to be written by hand. Writing books by hand took a long time, so books were rare and expensive. As more books were printed on printing presses, more people began to read. Soon it became fashionable to write books too. There were books on fishing, hunting, chess, medicine, art and travel. People could read about new ideas and so the new ideas began to spread. Explorers and traders could now buy accurate printed maps to help them navigate.

Did you know?

Some Europeans at this time were known as Renaissance Men. This meant that they studied lots of different subjects. Leonardo da Vinci (1452–1519) is a good example of a Renaissance Man. Find out where he was born, where he lived, who he worked for and what he is most famous for.

Be a good historian

Good historians look for as much detail as they can in images such paintings, drawings and photos. They look at everything in the images and read the caption and any labels carefully.

Activities

1 a What does the word 'Renaissance' mean? *rebirth*

   b Why do you think this period of European history is called the Renaissance?

2 Look at the picture of a printer's workshop on page 32. Look for: a man putting all the letters into sentences; the letters being covered in ink by pads; pages being printed in the printing press; printed pages drying; a child gathering together the printed pages to make a book; piles of printed pages.

   a Using all the details you have looked for in the picture, can you describe how books were printed during the Renaissance?

   b Why do you think historians have compared the invention of the printing press to the invention of the Internet?

Challenge

Find out about three important discoveries and inventions of the Renaissance period.

Answer these questions in your notebook.

Choose the best answer from the choices below. Write a, b or c as your answer.

1 About 1000 years ago, one of the largest cities in the world was:
   a New York
   b Baghdad
   c Paris

2 A scholar is a:
   a type of food
   b clever student
   c trader

3 The Ottoman tribe originally came from:
   a north-east Turkey
   b southern Spain
   c west Africa

4 The leading nations in the Age of Discovery and Exploration did not include:
   a Portugal
   b Hungary
   c Spain

5 The first European to sail around the southern tip of Africa and into the Indian Ocean was:
   a Vasco da Gama
   b Bartolomeu Dias
   c Christopher Columbus

6 Vasco da Gama become the first European to sail around Africa and land in India in:
   a 1478 CE
   b 1488 CE
   c 1498 CE

7 The name of the Spanish queen who sponsored Columbus's first voyage in 1492 CE was:
   a Queen Isabella
   b Queen Victoria
   c Queen Elizabeth

8 The disease caused by a lack of vitamin C that was common among sailors is:
   a chicken pox
   b scurvy
   c measles

9 The word 'Renaissance' translates as:
   a release
   b reactivate
   c rebirth

Decide if these statements are true or false. Write 'True' or 'False' for each one.

10 Many European traders began to look for new sea routes to India and the Far East because they did not want to pay the high taxes demanded by the Ottomans.

11 A caravel ship was between 100 and 150 metres long and weighed between 250 and 350 tonnes.

12 The crow's nest was where a sailor went to look for land.

13 The invention of the printing press meant that books could be produced slowly.

Now complete these tasks, writing no more than 100 words for each one.

14 Summarise the main points of the Golden Age in the Middle East.

15 Define the Age of Discovery and Exploration.

Now use the map to complete this task.

16 Using the map to help you, describe where Europeans explored during the Renaissance. Write as many reasons as you can to explain why Europeans began to explore and trade in different parts of the world during this time.

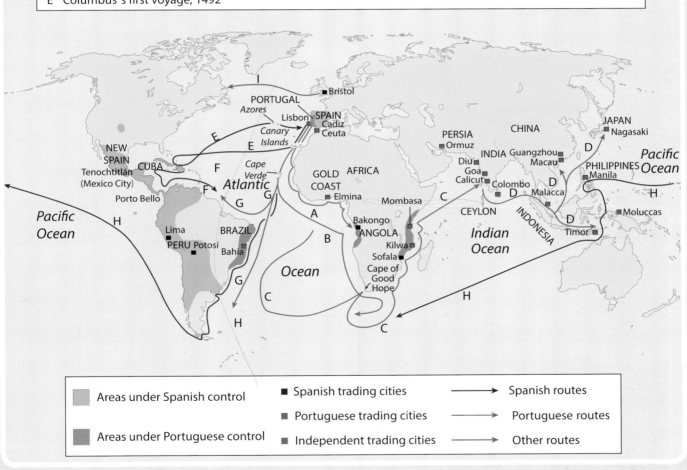

Principal Voyages of Exploration

A Portuguese expeditions, 1430s–1480s
B Dias, 1487–1488
C da Gama, 1497–1499
D Portuguese voyages to the Orient, 1509–1514
E Columbus's first voyage, 1492
F Columbus's three successive voyages, 1493–1504
G Voyages attended by Vespucci, 1499–1502
H Magellan–del Cano, 1519–1522
I Cabot, 1497

■ Areas under Spanish control   ■ Spanish trading cities   → Spanish routes
■ Areas under Portuguese control   ■ Portuguese trading cities   → Portuguese routes
   ■ Independent trading cities   → Other routes

In this unit you will:

- explain what it was like to live in Tudor times
- describe what a Tudor town looked like
- recall why and where the Tudors began to explore and trade
- explain how England changed in Tudor times

A painting from 1585 of Queen Elizabeth I, the Tudor Queen of England and daughter of King Henry VIII

? Look at the images on these photos and timeline. For how many years did the Tudors rule? What do the images tell us about the power and wealth of the Tudors?

Between 1485 CE and 1603 CE, a family called **Tudor** ruled England. This time in English history is known as the Tudor period. There were six Tudor **monarchs**, beginning with King Henry VII and ending with his granddaughter, Queen Elizabeth I.

symbol   Tudor
monarch   family tree
society   portrait

The Vikings
c700 CE–1100 CE

The Age of Discovery
and Exploration
c1400 CE–1600 CE

The Tudors
1485 CE–1603 CE

700 CE

1600 CE

The Tudors were the royal family in England from 1485 to 1603. This period was a time of great change. How did the Tudors take control of England? How were the Tudor kings and queens related? Who ruled England after the Tudors?

The Tudors take control

In the 1400s CE, England and Scotland were separate countries with different royal families. However, England controlled large areas of Ireland and Wales. Since the 12th century, the Plantagenet family had ruled England. In 1455, war broke out between two sides of the Plantagenet family. One side of the family was the House of Lancaster. The other side was the House of York. Both sides of the family wanted power. They fought for over 30 years.

In 1485, the leader of the House of Lancaster was Henry Tudor. At the Battle of Bosworth, Henry's army killed the leader of the House of York, Richard. Henry Tudor became Henry VII, the new King of England. He ended the wars between the two sides of the family by marrying Elizabeth, an important woman from the House of York.

Did you know?

A red rose was the symbol for the House of Lancaster and a white rose for the House of York. The wars between the two houses were known as the Wars of the Roses. Henry VII joined the two together and created the 'Tudor rose'.

Henry VII and Henry VIII

The son of Henry VII and Elizabeth of York became King of England in 1509 and was named Henry VIII. He married a Spanish princess named Catherine of Aragon. They had a daughter, Mary, born in 1516.

Henry VIII wanted a son to take over as king when he died. In England, there had never been a ruling queen. If Henry left only daughters when he died, he knew that rivals would challenge them for the throne.

So when Henry VIII thought that Catherine was too old to have any more children, he divorced her. They had been married for 23 years. Henry VIII married a younger woman, named Anne Boleyn.

Henry VIII and Anne Boleyn had a daughter, Elizabeth, in 1533. Henry was more desperate than ever to have a son. In 1536, Henry had Anne executed. He married for a third time. His new wife was named Jane Seymour. She gave birth to a boy, Edward, in 1537. However, Jane died soon after giving birth.

Henry VIII married three more times but he did not have any more children. Each of Henry's children – Mary, Elizabeth and Edward – ruled England at different times.

Be a good historian

Good historians are able to put events in the correct chronological order.

The family tree of the Tudor monarchs

Henry VII
King 1485–1509

Elizabeth of York: married in 1486

1
Married Catherine of Aragon in 1509

2
Married Anne Boleyn in 1533

3
Married Jane Seymour in 1536

Henry VIII
King 1509–1547

4
Married Anne of Cleves in 1540

5
Married Catherine Howard in 1540

6
Married Catherine Parr in 1543

Mary I
Queen 1553–1558

Elizabeth I
Queen 1558–1603

Edward VI
King 1547–1553

Henry VIII's children

After Henry VIII's death in 1547, his son Edward ruled. At this time, it was always the first-born son who became the next monarch, even if the daughters were older. Edward was only 9 years old when he became king, and he died at age 15 from a disease in his lungs. His oldest sister, Mary, became the next queen of England. Mary married King Philip II of Spain but they did not have any children. Mary died in 1558. Her younger sister, Elizabeth, became the next queen. Elizabeth ruled England for 44 years. Like her brother and sister, Elizabeth had no children. When Elizabeth died, her cousin James VI of Scotland inherited the English throne. He united both countries.

Activities

1 a Define the Wars of the Roses.

b How did the Wars of the Roses come to an end?

2 The following are all important years in the Tudor period:

1547   1509   1485   1516   1533

1603   1558   1553   1537   1536

a Write the years in the correct chronological order.

b Next to each year, write at least one fact about the Tudor royal family.

Challenge

Find out about the Scottish ruling family that replaced the Tudors. How was Elizabeth I related to James VI of Scotland? For how long did James VI rule? What was he like as a ruler? Who took over the throne from him?

In 1577 CE, a Tudor traveller named William Harrison wrote a book called *Description of England.* In this book, he wrote, 'we in England divide our people into four sorts: gentlemen, citizens, yeomen and labourers'. What did he mean? What was the difference between a gentleman and a yeoman? How was Tudor society organised?

Who were the gentlemen?

The gentlemen were the richest, most powerful people in Tudor **society**. They owned large areas of land and lived in huge houses in the countryside. They gave advice to the king or queen (if the royal person asked for advice) and helped the king or queen to run the country. Harrison described gentlemen as the 'princes, dukes, earls, barons and knights'. Gentlemen (and their wives and families) made up about 5 per cent of the population.

Who were the citizens?

The citizens lived in towns. They were also rich, but not as rich as the gentlemen. Many were merchants who made money from buying and selling goods such as wool, jewellery, food or cloth. They lived in large town houses and had servants. About 5 per cent of the population were citizens.

Who were the yeomen?

The yeomen were farmers. They either owned land or rented land from a gentleman. They often lived in a medium-sized farmhouse and made money from selling crops (such as wheat or barley) or livestock (such as cows and sheep).

A Tudor home: the people who lived here entertained guests with dinner parties, plays and music concerts.

Yeomen employed people to work on their farms and some yeomen had servants. Yeomen and their families made up about 30 per cent of the population.

'He eats well: bread and beef, good food – a full stomach. He works hard, his workers are happy to farm for him.'

Who were the labourers?

The labourers were poor. Most labourers lived in the countryside and worked on a farm for a yeoman. Some worked as servants. Some labourers owned a small piece of farmland to grow vegetables and to keep a few animals. The labourers who lived in towns made shoes, clothes, bricks, tools and furniture. Labourers made up about 60 per cent of the population.

Glossary words

labourer   museum   thatched

This Tudor town house is now used as shops and a **museum**.

'His house has walls of earth, a low thatched roof, few rooms, a hole in the wall to let out smoke. He is very poor and has to work hard for his living.'

An image from Tudor times

Did you know?

The population of England grew from about 2 million in 1520 CE to 4 million by 1600 CE.

Activities

1   Write a brief report of no more than 100 words with the title 'Description of England'. Your report should explain how the population of the country was divided into four groups within Tudor society.

2   Look at the three pictures and two descriptions on these pages. Can you match each picture and description to the correct group of people in Tudor society? Explain how you made your decisions.

Challenge

Find out about the types of food people ate in Tudor times. For example, what did rich people eat? How was this different from the food that poor people ate? What do the types of food that rich and poor people ate tell us about Tudor society? What types of food did merchants bring into England from abroad?

During Tudor times, many people moved from the countryside to towns in search of work. What was a Tudor town like?

Life in a Tudor town

Tudor towns were crowded, noisy and dirty. The streets were crammed with wooden houses, workshops and market stalls. Towns were centres of trade.

Farmers sold their crops and meat in large open-air markets. Merchants bought and sold goods such as fish, coal and cloth. Some merchants imported goods from abroad such as spices, silk and carpets. Many people got jobs in new industries such as glass-making, paper-making and book printing. Craftsmen such as metal-workers and shoemakers often had a shop on the ground floor of a house.

The front room of a house was often used as a shop.

People usually dumped their waste into the streets.

To save space, the houses were built very close together.

Merchants brought goods into the town to sell at the market.

The punishment for a minor crime was to lock the person in a wooden frame (called a 'pillory') for a few days.

Few people could read, so picture signs showed what the shops sold.

The streets were full of entertainers.

The streets were dirty. Disease was common.

Crime was common in towns. Thieves stole money and goods.

A busy street in a Tudor town

Tudor housing

Houses and shops were built with a wooden frame covered with bricks and plaster. The roof was covered with clay tiles. Servants slept at the very top of the house. The family lived and slept on the first floor. The kitchen, storeroom and shop were on the ground floor.

There was no running water – people got their water from a well. People usually dumped their household waste and rubbish into open sewers running through the streets. The dirty, crowded streets attracted fleas, flies and rats. Sickness and diseases were common and spread quickly.

Crime and punishment

There were no police in Tudor times. A man called a constable looked out for criminals. Another man, called a justice of the peace, settled disputes or sentenced criminals in court.

Tudor people believed that severe punishments would stop others from committing the same crimes, so punishments were harsh and brutal. Here are some examples.

- The punishment for stealing anything, even if it was worth very little, was hanging.

- The punishment for dishonest merchants was to drag them through the streets while people threw rubbish or rotten food at them.

- Beggars were whipped in the streets.

Did you know?

In Tudor times, 9 out of every 10 people lived in the countryside. Most of these people were farmers. They grew their own food and owned a few farm animals. If the farmers produced any extra food, they sold it at a market in the local town.

Activities

1   Imagine that you live in a town in Tudor times. Write a letter to a friend who lives in the countryside. Your letter should describe the Tudor town. For example, describe your house, the street you live on and the jobs people do in your town. Try to be as descriptive as possible – think about the sights, sounds and smells of a Tudor town as you write.

2   What are the main differences between a Tudor town and the town or city you live in today? Are there any similarities?

Challenge

Use books or the Internet to help you make a display or poster about Tudor London. For example, how big was Tudor London? How many people lived there? Find a map of Tudor London. Include some images of Tudor buildings that still survive today. Can you suggest reasons why some buildings have survived but other buildings have not survived?

Glossary words

import   sewers

There was no television or radio in Tudor times. People could not go to the cinema, play a computer game or download music. What entertainment was popular in Tudor times?

Entertainment for the rich

Rich people invited musicians and actors into their homes. Rich people watched plays and danced to music. They also enjoyed jousting, hunting, bowling and playing chess.

Jousting is a contest in which two men on horseback try to knock each other off their horses with a long pole.

Fun, games and sports

Poorer people had hard lives and worked very long hours. When they had any spare time, they made sure they had lots of fun. Singing, dancing, fishing and archery were popular. Jugglers and acrobats travelled from village to village and entertained people for a few coins. People also watched bears fighting with dogs.

Glossary words

jousting   theatre   tournament

Poorer people played an early type of football. Crowds of people from one village or town played against people from another village or town. The players carried, kicked and threw the ball across land between the villages. The winners were the team that got the ball to the centre of the other village. The game often continued for many hours and was very violent. In 1602 CE, a spectator wrote about the game: 'The players go home as if they have been at war, with bleeding heads and broken bones'.

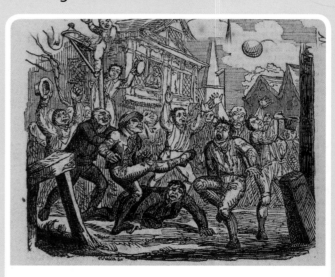

A picture of a football match in Tudor times

A trip to the theatre

Watching plays at a theatre became very popular during Tudor times. Both rich and poor people enjoyed a visit to the theatre. The theatres were usually round and the roof did not always cover the whole building. The richer people sat in covered seats on each side, while poorer people stood in an open area, called the pit. By 1595 in London, 15 000 people a week watched plays.

A flag was flown or a trumpet was blown to announce the start of a play.

tectum

Richer people sat under cover in the gallery.

porticus

orchestra

mimorum aedes

The stage

proscenium

There were no female actors. All characters were played by men or boys.

Poorer people stood here. They laughed at the jokes or shouted if they did not like the play.

Food and drink were served here.

planities siue arena.

ex obseruationibus Londinensibus Iohannis de witt

This picture shows the inside of the Swan Theatre in London, which was built in 1595 CE.

Did you know?

King Henry VIII was a keen sportsman. He enjoyed archery, wrestling and tennis. He was also a keen jouster and was badly injured at a tournament in January 1536 when he was thrown from his horse. He was unconscious for two hours.

Be a good historian

Good historians understand that learning about the lives of ordinary people is just as important as learning about the lives of kings and queens.

Activities

1 Look at the picture of jousting on page 44. Why do you think that only richer people took part in jousting?

2 Write a conversation between two people in Tudor England. One person has never been to a theatre, but the other person has. The person who has never been to the theatre should ask questions and the other person should answer them.

3 In what ways is the modern game of football different from football played in Tudor times? Are there any similarities?

Challenge

Theatres were very popular in Tudor times. William Shakespeare became famous for writing plays. Find out about the life of William Shakespeare and the plays he wrote. Which other people are famous for writing plays in Tudor times?

A Tudor child's education depended on how rich the child's father was. Some poorer children did spend some time in school learning to read and write, but a high-quality education was usually only for the wealthy. How were children educated? How long was a school day? What were the lessons like?

Rich and poor

Some towns and villages had a small school where poorer children were taught to read and write for a few hours each week. These schools were free. When children were old enough to help on the farm or learn a trade they stopped going to school.

1 School rules: Tudor schools were very strict. Students could be whipped for being late, not learning to spell properly or forgetting a book. The richest children paid for a 'whipping-boy'. When the rich child was naughty, the whipping-boy received the punishment.

2 The birch: the students were whipped with this. A 'birch' was a bundle of thin branches (from a birch tree) tied together.

3 A portrait: a painting of the king, queen or founder of the school was on display.

4 Books: students had to bring their own books to school. Books were very expensive in Tudor times.

5 Girls in school: it was not common to see girls in school. Most rich girls were educated at home.

6 As well as Latin, pupils learned Greek, religion and mathematics. Children wrote with a quill pen, made from a feather, and they read from a hornbook.

7 Teacher: some schools were small, with just one or two rooms and one teacher. The teacher was sometimes called a 'school master'.

8 Toys and games: the students played with balls, hoops and other games during break times.

The richest families paid a tutor to teach their children at home. Rich children who did not have a tutor went to a grammar school. These schools were called grammar schools because the students were taught lots of Latin grammar. Latin was the language that businessmen and merchants used throughout Europe. Most books at the time were written in Latin too. Ambitious fathers wanted their children to learn Latin grammar, and were prepared to pay a lot of money to make sure their children received a good education. Children went to grammar school at the age of 7. The cleverest children then went to study at university when they were 14 or 15 years old. There were two universities in Tudor England: Oxford and Cambridge.

Look at the picture on page 46 and read the labels. The picture shows what a grammar school might have looked like in Tudor times.

6.00 a.m.	Day starts with Latin grammar
8.00 a.m.	Mathematics
10.00 a.m.	Greek grammar
12:00 noon	Lunch: bread, cheese, beef, dried fruit
1.00 p.m.	Essays
2.00 p.m.	Religious studies
3.00 p.m.	English
4.00 p.m.	Homework time
4.45 p.m.	Prayers
5.00 p.m.	Home

A typical school timetable: Tudor students attended school six days a week, Monday to Saturday.

Glossary words

| grammar school | quill pen |
| hornbook | the past |

Activities

1 Why did very few children from poor families go to school in Tudor times?

2 Write a list of similarities and differences between your school and a school in Tudor times.

3 Imagine that you are a student at the school described on these pages. Write a diary entry for a typical day in this school.

Challenge

Find out about the oldest school in your area or country. How old is it? How has the school changed over the years?

Be a good historian

Good historians know that some things about the past are very similar to the way things are today, and other things are very different. There are many things about Tudor schools that are similar to schools today, and lots of things that are different.

There were no cameras in Tudor times. All images of Tudor kings and queens were either painted or drawn. Tudor kings and queens wanted people to think they were powerful, rich and wise. They carefully controlled each picture so it did not make them look old or weak. They made sure that the artist filled the painting or drawing with symbols that showed the king or queen's power, achievements and wealth. What do these portraits of Queen Elizabeth I tell us?

Investigating Elizabeth's image

Look carefully at these three **portraits** of Henry VIII's daughter, Elizabeth. The first portrait, below, was painted in 1574 CE.

The second portrait was painted in 1588 shortly after the English defeated the Spanish Armada.

The crown shows that Elizabeth is a queen.

This collar, known as a ruff, was very fashionable.

Elizabeth's white make-up showed that she was very rich and did not have to work, so she was never dirty.

The Spanish ships after they have been defeated.

Pearls were a symbol for purity and wealth.

Here, the painting shows the arrival of the Spanish ships.

Elizabeth is pointing to America, where English people were beginning to settle. Her fingers are spread across other parts of the world – what could this mean?

The richest people wore black clothing.

This type of headdress was very fashionable.

Pearls were a symbol for purity.

She has a pelican on her necklace. Pelicans are known to be protective of their young. Elizabeth wanted to protect the people of her country.

The Tudor roses on her silk dress show her connection to the Tudor family.

The gold and precious stones were symbols for wealth.

This gold fan was both fashionable and expensive.

The colours red, black and gold were only worn by the highest classes.

The third portrait was painted in about 1600.

Elizabeth was over 60 years old when this picture was painted. The long hair is a symbol for youth and long life.

The headdress is covered in jewels to show wealth.

Flowers were a symbol of youth.

Can you see the eyes and ears on the cloak? Elizabeth is trying to show that she can see and hear everything.

The rainbow shows that Elizabeth is bringing peace after stormy times.

A snake was a symbol of intelligence and good judgment.

Controlling the paintings

Elizabeth wanted the paintings of herself to impress people. She took a great interest in the paintings and always told the artist to change a painting if she was unhappy with any of the details. No paintings of the queen were allowed unless she approved them.

Glossary word

armada

Activities

1   Write a guide book for visitors to the gallery where these three portraits were on display. Include information about Queen Elizabeth I, when the portraits were painted and what the portraits try to tell us about her.

2   Use the Internet or books to find a portrait of another ruler in a different part of the world. Write a fact file about this ruler and explain how the painter has attempted to portray the ruler. Here are some ideas of portraits you could look for:

Suleiman the Magnificent, who ruled the Ottoman Empire from 1520 to his death in 1566

Emperor Longqing or Emperor Jiajing of the Chinese Ming dynasty

Emperor Akbar or Emperor Humayun of the Mughal Empire in India.

Challenge

Use books and the Internet to find some written descriptions of Queen Elizabeth I. How do the written descriptions compare with the portraits of Elizabeth?

Answer these questions in your notebook.

Choose the best answer from the choices below. Write a, b or c as your answer.

1 The wars between different parts of the royal family in the 1400s CE were known as the:
   a Wars of the Flowers
   b Wars of the Roses
   c Wars of the Crown

2 The name of the first Tudor king was:
   a Henry VII
   b Henry VIII
   c Richard III

3 Henry VIII's second wife was:
   a Anne Boleyn
   b Jane Seymour
   c Catherine Howard

4 The percentage of people who were poor labourers in Tudor times was:
   a 60 per cent
   b 50 per cent
   c 70 per cent

5 The richest, most powerful people in Tudor times were:
   a yeomen
   b gentlemen
   c citizens

6 A sport that was not popular in Tudor times was:
   a jousting
   b football
   c basketball

7 Most Tudor theatres were:
   a square
   b round
   c rectangular

8 Schools for richer children were called grammar schools because:
   a grammar was a Tudor name for a teacher
   b students were taught mainly Latin grammar
   c students had to pass a grammar exam to be accepted by the school

9 In Tudor schools, students wrote with a quill pen. These pens were made from:
   a a tree branch
   b an animal bone
   c a feather

Rewrite these sentences so that they are correct.

10 Henry VIII had three children – two daughters named Mary and Eleanor and a son named Edward.

11 Henry VIII married eight times.

12 In Tudor times, household waste was collected from homes and taken away for recycling.

13 There were three universities in Tudor England: Oxford, Cambridge and York.

Now complete these tasks.

14 Answer the following questions about Henry VIII.
   a Who was Henry VIII's father?
   b What was the name of Henry VIII's mother?
   c Write the names of Henry VIII's three children. Next to each name, write the name of that child's mother.
   d Write the names of Henry VIII's three wives who did not have children.

e Write the names of Henry VIII's wives in the correct order of marriage, beginning with the wife he married first and ending with the one he married last.

f How has King Henry VIII been portrayed in this painting? What do you think Henry wanted people to think when they looked at this portrait?

15 Read these two descriptions of Queen Elizabeth I carefully, then answer the questions that follow.

'On her head she wore a great red wig. Her face appears to be very aged. It is long and thin. Her teeth are yellow and unequal and there are less on the left than on the right. Many of them are missing and one cannot understand her easily when she speaks. She is tall and graceful.'

A French visitor, describing Elizabeth in 1597, when she was 64 years old. This was six years before her death.

'Her face is oblong, fair but wrinkled; her eyes small yet black and pleasant; her nose is a little hooked; her lips narrow and her teeth black. She wears false red hair; her hands are small, her fingers long and her height neither tall nor short.'

A French visitor's description of Elizabeth in 1598

a Write down all the details in the descriptions of Elizabeth I that the two writers agree on.

b What do the two writers not agree on?

c Suggest reasons why the two writers disagree on certain details.

d Why do you think portrait painters did not include in Elizabeth's portrait some of the details mentioned by the writers?

3 The Tudors

In this unit you will:

- explain who first settled in London and why
- describe how and why London grew so rapidly
- recall how plagues, fires and invasions had a major impact on London
- explain the history behind some of London's most famous buildings
- summarise how London has changed and continues to develop

43 CE
The Romans arrived in Britain. They built a bridge over the River Thames.

61 CE
London was burned down by enemies of the Roman invaders. It was quickly rebuilt.

410 CE
The Romans left Britain. New tribes invaded Britain (and London).

886 CE
London became the capital of Britain.

1078 CE
The Tower of London's central tower was built.

1240 CE
The first parliament m in London.

Over the past 2000 years, London has been the site of invasions, **plagues**, fires and warfare. Today, London is one of the largest and most famous cities in the world.

> plague
> **Industrial Revolution**
> **Blitz**   rebuild

? Look at the timeline. Which do you think are the most significant events in London's history? Choose three events and explain why you made these choices.

65 CE
e Great
ague killed
e fifth of the
opulation.

1666 CE
The Great Fire destroyed 80 per cent of London's buildings.

1735 CE
10 Downing Street became the home of Britain's prime minister.

1829 CE
Britain's first police force was established in London.

1837–1870 CE
The current Houses of Parliament were built.

1939–1945 CE
World War Two. Children were evacuated, and London was heavily bombed.

Almost 2000 years ago, the Romans invaded Britain. They came to Britain looking for land, slaves and precious metals such as iron, lead, zinc, copper, silver and gold. They built a town beside the River Thames – and this town became London. Why did the Romans choose to build London in this place? What did Roman London look like? How many people lived in London at this time?

Glossary words

invade	port

The location of London

After the Romans invaded Britain in 43 CE, they built a bridge across the River Thames where London is located today. However, they did not settle there or build a town immediately. In about 50 CE, the Romans decided that it was an excellent place to build a port. The River Thames was deep enough for larger trading ships but it was far enough inland to be safe from attacks from foreign tribes. The Romans also believed it was a good place from which to build roads to every part of Britain.

The first thing the Romans did was build a fort. Then, Roman merchants, helped by the Roman army, built a town next to the bridge. The Romans called the town Londinium, and we know it today as London.

London under threat

Early Roman London was surrounded by a large ditch and a strong wooden fence. Roman soldiers patrolled the edge of the town in case of attack by British tribes. In 61 CE, while the main Roman army was busy in Wales, a British tribe, the Iceni, attacked London. The Iceni tribe was unhappy that the Romans were taking more and more of their land. Queen Boudicca led her tribe into battle and they burned London down. The Roman army soon raced back to defeat Queen Boudicca, but London was in ruins.

London is rebuilt

The Romans quickly **rebuilt** London. They replaced the old wooden houses that had burned down with houses built of stone. Soon London became the largest town in Britain, with a population of about 45 000.

The boats on the river. London was an important port for the Romans. Luxury goods such as olive oil, glass, fine pottery, silk and ivory were imported from all over the Roman Empire. The Romans exported grain and metals from Britain.

The largest building was called the forum and basilica. This building was over 30 metres wide and 140 metres long. It was used as both a town hall and a shopping centre.

The stone wall surrounding London

This is what London might have looked like in Roman times.

London contained everything a citizen of Roman Britain needed – houses, shops, markets, meeting places, workshops, offices and temples. A stone wall six metres high was built around the city for protection.

Most of the Roman wall around London has been destroyed or removed over time. Small sections remain, surrounded by modern buildings.

The Romans leave

In 410 CE, the Romans left Britain. They went to defend their lands from attack in other parts of Europe. London was abandoned and fell into ruin. Then Anglo-Saxon tribes invaded Britain and began to settle. They built a new town along the River Thames to the west of London called Lundenwic, which became a busy port. However, Lundenwic was defenceless against invasions from the Vikings. So, in 886 CE, the Anglo-Saxon King Alfred moved people back into London. Here, people were safer because they were protected by the strong, stone Roman walls. Soon, London began to thrive again.

Activities

1   Imagine you were a Roman soldier based in London in 70 CE. Write a letter to your family in Rome, telling them:
    a   why the Romans chose to settle in London
    b   what London looks like (describe the town)
    c   why London is under threat and why a wall has been built.

2   Work with a friend or in a small group to carry out research into one of the following cities to find out how it has developed over time.
    ● New York City, USA   ● Tokyo, Japan   ● Rio de Janeiro, Brazil
    ● Paris, France   ● Nairobi, Kenya   ● Cairo, Egypt

3   Prepare a presentation on your chosen city's development. When was the city founded – and why? How has it changed over time? What big events have affected the city?

Challenge

In London, builders and archeologists have uncovered many Roman objects. Use the information on these two pages and further research to create a presentation about some of the objects that have been found.

From the time the Romans left Britain (410 CE) to the time of the Tudor kings and queens (1485 CE) is a period of about 1000 years. In the history of Europe, this period of time is often called the Middle Ages. How did London change during this time?

The slow growth of London

After the Romans left, London was empty for many years. The new invaders, the Anglo-Saxons, did not like living in Roman towns. They preferred to live in wooden homes in smaller villages. Over time, however, people slowly began to move back into London, which was protected by huge stone walls. The port grew busy again and the city was full of industry: brick-making and pottery, metal-working, weaving and leather-working. There was also a mint, built in 886 CE during the reign of the Anglo-Saxon King Alfred, which made silver coins.

Invasion

In 1066 CE, William the Conqueror came from Normandy in France to invade England. He defeated King Harold, the last Anglo-Saxon king, and was crowned king of England in London on Christmas Day 1066. To impress and control the local English people, in 1078 the king starting building a large castle next to the River Thames. The Tower of London, as it became known, was not just a place where the king could feel safe, it was also used as a prison, a treasury and a weapons store. William the Conqueror and his family also built many other buildings in London.

The Tower of London: after William the Conqueror, later kings added towers and other features. It is now one of the most popular tourist attractions in Britain.

A busy place

In the Middle Ages, London was a maze of narrow, twisting streets and lanes. It was also a very dirty place. A single open sewer ran down the middle of each street and people tipped their rubbish here. When it rained, the rubbish was washed into the River Thames. Illness and disease were common. Between 1348 and 1665 CE, there were at least 16 outbreaks of a deadly disease called the plague. Sometimes the outbreaks of plague killed thousands of people.

Most of the houses were made from wood so there was always the risk of fire. Laws were passed to make sure all houses contained fire-fighting equipment.

Many of the streets in London were named after the main product that was traded there, for example, Bread Street and Honey Lane. Cows were kept for milking on Milk Street. All of these streets still exist today.

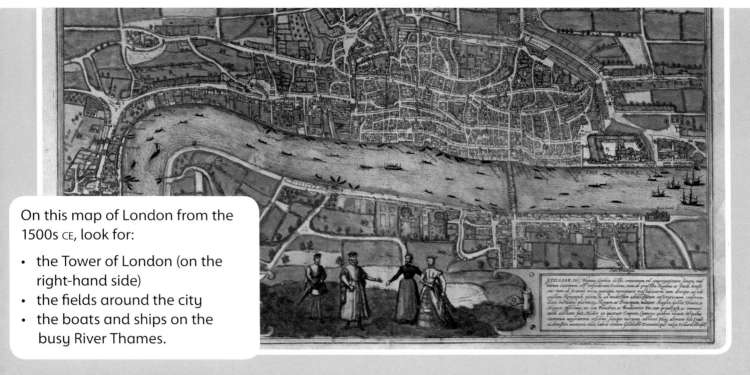

On this map of London from the 1500s CE, look for:

- the Tower of London (on the right-hand side)
- the fields around the city
- the boats and ships on the busy River Thames.

Glossary words

mint reign

Activities

1 Using the information in this book, answer the following questions.

   a Why did the Anglo-Saxon tribes not move into London when the Romans left?

   b Why did William the Conqueror build the Tower of London?

   c Look at the picture of the Tower of London. Describe the building.

   d Read the written description of London from the 12th century CE. Where in London could you buy fish? Where could you buy sheep?

2 You have been asked to write part of a book about London. You will write a section called 'London in the Middle Ages'. Write no more than 100 words.

Read the extract below to find out about items traded in London.

' Traders can be found in their area each morning. There is fish for sale on the river bank. Every day you may find food, dishes of meat — roast, fried and boiled; fish; cheap cuts of meat for the poor and more expensive for the rich…. Just outside the town there is a field called Smithfield. On every sixth day of the week there is a sale of fine horses, farming tools, milk, cows, large oxen and sheep. '

From a description of London in the 12th century CE, written by William Fitz Stephen

Challenge

Use information in this book and further research to write what you think are the 10 most interesting facts about the Tower of London.

In September 1666 CE, a huge fire burned down most of London. By now, London was one of the largest cities in the world. The fire was so big that it was called the Great Fire of London – and it changed the city forever. How did the fire start? Why was it so devastating? How did London change as a result of the fire?

The fire begins

In the early hours of Sunday 2 September 1666, a baker named Thomas Farriner was woken by smoke coming under the door of his bedroom. Downstairs in his bakery in Pudding Lane, a fire had started and his house had caught fire. Farriner, with his wife and daughter, managed to escape out of an upstairs window. His maid, who lived with them, was not so lucky. She refused to follow them out of the window because she was frightened of falling into the street. She died in the fire, and was the first victim of the Great Fire of London.

The fire spreads

The fire spread very quickly. Most of the houses in London were made of wood, so they burned easily. There had been a drought in London during the summer, so all the wood was very dry. Also, houses were built close together along London's narrow streets.

This meant that the fire was able to move easily and quickly from one house to the next. By early morning, about 300 houses had been destroyed – and strong winds carried the flames towards more and more buildings.

Panic!

The people of London were terrified. The streets were filled with frightened people. Many people tried to leave the city as quickly as possible. Some went to the River Thames and paid boat owners to take them away.

> ' Poor people stayed in their houses until the fire touched them, and then ran into boats or climbed from one set of stairs to another. And among other things, the poor birds did not want to leave and hovered by the windows and balconies until they burned their wings and fell down. '

Samuel Pepys, who kept a diary at the time, wrote about the impact of the fire on both the people of London and the wildlife.

Glossary word

fire-break

Fighting the fire

Some people carried water from the river in leather buckets to throw at the flames. King Charles II went into the city and ordered some houses to be pulled down to make a fire-break. However, the flames were so hot that the piles of wood and plaster caught fire too. The street itself was so hot that people burned their feet as they ran.

The fire began to die down on Wednesday 5 September 1666. By now, thousands of people had set up camps in the fields around London because their homes had been destroyed. In total, the fire destroyed 13 000 houses and many important buildings. At least 100 000 people were now homeless.

The fire spread quickly between the wooden houses. Many people escaped in boats on the River Thames.

Activities

1 Write a detailed report on the Great Fire of London. In your report, include information such as when the fire started, who the first victim was, how and why the fire spread so quickly, and how people tried to fight the fire.

2 Samuel Pepys's diary is full of information about life in London at this time.

   a Why are diaries a very useful source of information for historians?

   b Can you suggest reasons why people's diaries are sometimes not the most reliable source of information for historians?

Did you know?

In 2014, archeologists tested a melted piece of pottery found in Pudding Lane. Their tests showed that the Great Fire of London reached a temperature of 1250°C in Pudding Lane. That is slightly hotter than the average temperature of lava from a volcano!

Challenge

London is not the only city that has been destroyed by a fire. Rome, Tokyo, San Francisco and Chicago have each been destroyed by 'great fires' in the past. Find out about other 'great fires' in history. When did they happen? What caused them? How destructive were they? How did the cities change as a result of these fires?

A new London

The Great Fire destroyed about 80 per cent of London. Now the city had to be rebuilt. The government said that the newly built houses had to be made from brick and stone, instead of wood. There were also limits on the height of new houses and they were not allowed to be built so close together. This picture shows a new London street built near to where the fire started. You will notice that the street is wide and the houses are made from stone.

A London street built after the Great Fire

Glossary words

government   monument

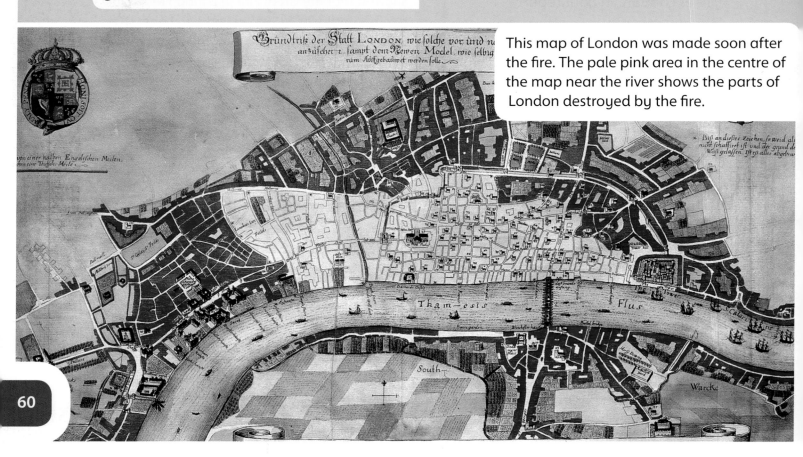

This map of London was made soon after the fire. The pale pink area in the centre of the map near the river shows the parts of London destroyed by the fire.

The monument to the Great Fire

The Great Fire has its own monument, which still exists today and attracts over 160 000 visitors per year. It is a large, hollow stone column that stands just over 61 metres tall. You can climb 311 steps inside to reach a viewing platform that has fantastic views over London. There is even a London Underground train station called Monument.

The Monument, London. It is just over 61 metres tall for a reason – if it was laid on its side, it would reach the spot in Pudding Lane where the Great Fire started.

Did you know?

The exact number of people killed in the fire is unknown, but traditionally it is thought to be only between six and ten people. Immediately after the event, rumours spread that French spies had started the fire. One French visitor was attacked with an iron bar and another had his furniture smashed by angry Londoners.

Activities

1   Use the information in this book and further research to answer these questions about the Great Fire of London.

   a   How much of London was destroyed by the fire?

   b   How did London change as a result of the Great Fire?

   c   What is the Monument? Why was it built where it stands today? Why is it 61 metres tall?

2   Design your own monument to the Great Fire. Draw your design, then describe where you will place your monument and what materials it will be made from. Give reasons for your chosen design.

Challenge

What other monuments do you know? Is there one in your local area, town or capital city? Carry out some research using the Internet, a library or a museum. When was the monument built? Why was it built? Was it built to remind people of a person or an event?

Be a good historian

Good historians can identify what are called 'turning points' in history. These are key events, inventions or developments that changed things completely.

In the 200 years after the Great Fire, London was transformed into the world's largest city. It became a global centre for trade and industry. The population rose from about 600 000 in 1700 to about 1 million in 1800. By 1900, London's population had grown to 6 million. Why and how did London change during this period?

Changing times

In the late 1700s and 1800s, Britain went through a period known as the **Industrial Revolution**. At this time, the production of goods moved from small shops and houses into large factories. Farming was still an important industry, but coal, iron, steel and cloth also became very important. Some people made huge fortunes in these industries. It was also a time of great technological change that saw important developments in transport, medical knowledge and communication.

In Britain, towns and cities grew rapidly at this time, as people moved from the countryside to look for work in one of the many new factories and businesses. In 1745, for example, 80 per cent of people in Britain lived and worked in the countryside. By 1900, 80 per cent lived and worked in towns and cities.

Be a good historian

Good historians know that people's lives can be very different, even if they live in the same town or city in the same period of history. Write a paragraph to describe the differences between the lives of rich people and poor people in London in the 19th century.

' Food and drink were important industries. There were flour mills and sauce factories in Lambeth and sugar refineries in Whitehall and St Georges in the East. The first tinned foods were made in Bermondsey. Bermondsey and Southwark were famous for their leather industry and for hat making. Bethnal Green was noted for boot and shoe making. The clothing trade was also important. Chemicals were made in Silvertown and West Ham. Clocks and watches and jewellery were made in Clerkenwell. There were shipyards in Poplar, Deptford, Millwall and Blackwall. Other industries in London included furniture making, machine and tool making and the manufacture of horse drawn carriages.

A description of London's industry in the 19th century by Tim Lambert

London – a centre of trade and industry

London became a huge manufacturing centre at this time, making the vast amount of goods that Britain's growing population wanted. During the 1700s and 1800s, Britain's empire also grew. By 1900, Britain ruled over about 450 million people living in 56 areas (or colonies) around the world. The British Empire contained one quarter of the world's population and covered one quarter of the Earth's total land area. The British Empire was controlled from London. The city's port area also grew rapidly at this time, importing and exporting goods from all over the British Empire.

Glossary words

docks   import   export

A changing city

In the 1800s, many of London's most famous buildings were built – Buckingham Palace was completed in 1850, the Houses of Parliament were built between 1837 and 1870, and Tower Bridge opened in 1894. London's famous railways stations (Euston, King's Cross and St. Pancras) were built between 1837 and 1868, and the first underground railway opened in 1863.

In the 19th century, London was a city of extremes. The richer people lived on the edges of London in larger houses, while the poorer workers lived near to the factories and docks in the centre of the city. In poorer areas, such as the East End, whole families were crowded into one room of a house. These houses were cold, damp, dark and dirty. Sometimes a pump provided water, but the water usually came from the local river, which was filthy. There were no rubbish collections, litter bins, street cleaners, sewers or fresh running water.

These two photos show the differences between rich and poor in London in the 19th century. The photos were taken at about the same time, only a few miles apart, in different areas of London.

Activities

1. **a** What was the Industrial Revolution?
   b How were the Industrial Revolution and the British Empire linked to the growth of London?

2. Look at the two photos above.
   a Describe each photo.
   b Decide which photo shows the rich area of London and which photo shows the poor area. What details in the photos helped you decide?

3. Use the Internet to find a map of London in about 1850. Compare it to the map on page 60 of this book. What has changed? What has not changed? Can you explain these changes?

Challenge

You may have found out about many empires in your studies in history (the Roman Empire and British Empire, for example). Find out five facts about five different empires in history. Make sure you present your research on the empires in the correct chronological order.

During World War Two, London was bombed in a series of air attacks known as the Blitz. Thousands of people were killed, injured and made homeless, and large parts of the city were destroyed. What was it like to live through the Blitz? How much of London was destroyed? How did London change after the war?

London before World War Two

London continued to grow rapidly in the early 20th century. Large housing estates were built on the edges of the city and new industries such as car-making, electronics and aircraft manufacturing employed thousands of people. London's population rose from 6 million in 1900 to 8.5 million by 1939.

The Blitz

During World War Two, Hitler and his German forces tried to take over the whole of Europe. Hitler succeeded in gaining control of many countries, including France, Denmark, Poland, Norway and Belgium. He hoped to invade Britain in September 1940, but when his plans to destroy Britain's air force failed, he changed tactics and launched huge bombing raids on Britain's cities instead. He hoped that Britain would surrender because of these raids.

The first bombing raid came on 7 September 1940 when 1000 German warplanes dropped thousands of bombs on London.

A London bus lies buried in a bomb crater, the morning after a German air raid in October 1940.

The raids continued for the next nine months, during which time over 20 000 Londoners were killed and over 25 000 were injured. More than 1 million London houses were destroyed or damaged. Other British towns and cities were also bombed. The British responded by bombing German towns and cities too.

The **Blitz** eventually ended when the Germans changed their plans and decided to use their bomber planes for the invasion of Russia in 1941.

London rebuilds

Just before the war, the government said that London had become overcrowded. When the war ended, the government revealed plans to relocate Londoners from poor-quality or bombed-out housing. About 20–30 miles from London, 10 new towns were built. As well as new towns, a series of high-rise apartments (known as flats) were built. The landscape of London changed after the war, when many tall buildings, up to 25 storeys high, appeared all over the city.

Glossary words

apartment	housing estate	tourism
flat	shelter	

A German bomber plane flies over the dock area of London near the River Thames during the Blitz.

After the war, modern houses and flats were built to replace the homes that had been destroyed. Today, London is a mix of old and new buildings.

After the end of the war, London's trade and industry changed greatly. Industries such as car-making and aircraft making, engineering and electronics went into decline, while banking, tourism and construction flourished.

London's population decreased after the war, despite the arrival of many thousands of immigrants from the West Indies, Pakistan, India, Africa and China, for example. Many of the immigrants were from former colonies of the British Empire. However, in the last years of the 20th century, London's population began to rise again as people moved into the city looking for work. In the early years of the 21st century, the population was about 8 million.

Did you know?

About 150 000 Londoners sheltered in underground train stations during the bombing raids of World War Two. In parts of London and in other cities, some people built shelters in their gardens. Other people left the cities and went to the safer countryside areas.

Activities

1   Write a brief fact file about London since 1900. Include: London's population, the Blitz, London since World War Two and the new housing estates. Choose two images to include in your fact file.

2   Use books and the Internet to find out how London's population has changed over time. Draw a line graph to present your findings.

Challenge

Carry out research to find out the top 10 tourist attractions in London today. Mark them on a map of the city. How many people visit each attraction each year? Why do you think these attractions are so popular?

④ Review

Answer these questions in your notebook.

Choose the best answer from the choices below. Write a, b or c as your answer.

1 In 61 CE, the people of the Iceni tribe were unhappy that the Romans were taking more and more of their land. They attacked London and burned down the city. The tribe was led by:
  a Queen Latifa
  b Queen Boudicca
  c Queen Elizabeth

2 During Roman times, what was the estimated population of London?
  a 45 000
  b 55 000
  c 65 000

3 The famous London building, built on the orders of William the Conqueror, was:
  a The Tower of London
  b Tower Bridge
  c Buckingham Palace

4 The Great Fire of London started on:
  a 22 September 1666
  b 2 September 1666
  c 2 September 1665

5 The Great Fire started in a:
  a clothing shop on Threadneedle Street
  b shoe shop next to the River Thames
  c bakery on Pudding Lane

6 The percentage of London destroyed in the Great Fire was:
  a 60 per cent
  b 70 per cent
  c 80 per cent

7 London's population reached 1 million in:
  a 1800
  b 1850
  c 1900

8 London's port area grew rapidly during the 1700s and 1800s, when the British Empire was at its height. At this time, the number of areas (known as colonies) that the British controlled was:
  a 46
  b 56
  c 66

9 The name given to the series of German bombing attacks on London during World War Two was:
  a the Big Bang
  b the Crash
  c the Blitz

Decide if these statements are true or false. Write 'True' or 'False' for each one.

12 Many London streets were named after the main product that was traded there.

13 The Anglo-Saxons were the first to build a bridge across the River Thames.

Now complete these tasks.

14 Use books and the Internet to find out what Samuel Pepys wrote about the Great Plague, a deadly disease that hit London in 1665, the year before the Great Fire. What did Pepys think caused the plague? When did he first hear about it? How many Londoners died in the plague?

15 In history, a 'turning point' is a significant moment when something begins to change. A turning point can be an event, a development or an invention, for example. Identify three turning points in London's history, which changed London forever. Explain why you have chosen them.

10 When London was under attack during World War Two, many people sheltered in:
  a the Tower of London
  b Buckingham Palace
  c the London Underground

11 After World War Two ended, the government built new towns outside London to replace poor-quality and bombed-out housing. The number of towns built was:
  a 30
  b 20
  c 10

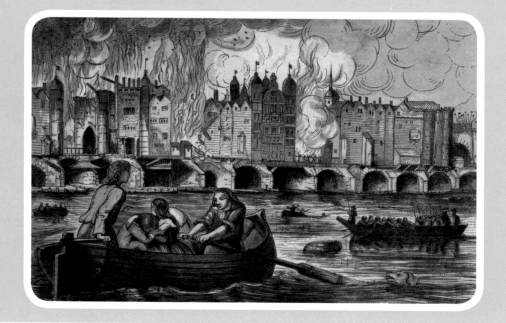

Vocabulary quiz

Answer these questions in your notebook.

1 The Vikings

1   Write what type of boat this picture shows. Then write the labels for each part of the boat a–e.

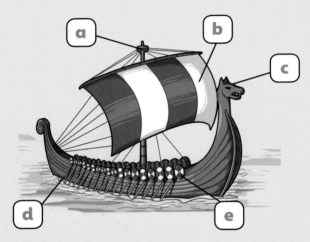

2   Which is the odd one out in each group of words? Explain your answer.

   a   farming   meeting   fishing   hunting
   b   fur   wool   timber   thrall
   c   Denmark   Norway   Russia   Sweden

3   Write a definition for each of the following words. Then use each word correctly in a sentence or short paragraph.

   a   navigator
   b   warrior
   c   inherit
   d   Thing
   e   outlaw
   f   saga

2 The Age of Discovery and Exploration

1   a   Sort the words below in a table.

Life at sea	Trade goods	The Renaissance

   caravel   experiments   honey
   indigo   printing press   scholars
   scurvy   spices   watch

   b   Add at least one new word to each group.

2   Write what each of these pictures shows. Then write a sentence or short paragraph to explain how each of these items was used during the Age of Discovery and Exploration.

   a      b

   c

3   Write a definition for each of these words. Then use each word correctly in a sentence or short paragraph.

   a   explorer   c   scholar
   b   Middle Ages   d   Renaissance

3 The Tudors

1 Match the words with the definitions.

 a a king, queen or emperor

 b the period of time when one king or queen rules

 c the period of English history between 1485 CE and 1603 CE

 d an object that represents something else

 e all the people living in a country, with shared traditions, laws, interests and activities

 f a diagram that shows how people in a family are related to each other

> family tree   monarch   reign
> society   symbol   Tudor

2 Which is the odd one out in each group of words? Explain your answer.

 a sewers gentlemen yeomen labourers

 b Latin theatre Greek mathematics

 c jousting football hunting museum

3 Write a definition for each of these words. Then use each word correctly in a sentence or short paragraph.

 a Armada

 b portrait

 c tournament

 d hornbook

 e grammar school

 f quill pen

4 The story of London

1 Choose the word that matches each definition.

 a a place where money is made

> port   mint   museum

 b a deadly disease that killed many people

> Blitz   drought   plague

 c to sell goods to other countries

> export   import   report

 d the group of people who make the laws in a country

> government   empire   society

a  b  c

2 Write what each of these pictures shows. Then use each word correctly in a sentence or short paragraph.

3 Look at these groups of words about four different times in London's history. Write a short paragraph about each of these times using all of the words in the group.

 a **Roman London:** bridge, fort, tribe, rebuild

 b **The Great Fire:** smoke, narrow, river, fire-break

 c **The Industrial Revolution:** industry, factories, businesses, docks

 d **World War Two:** raids, Blitz, bombs, shelter

Glossary

adventure an exciting or dangerous journey

apartment a set of rooms for living in, usually on one floor of a building

archeologist a person who studies objects and sites from the past to learn about human history

armada a large fleet of ships

armour clothing that is worn to protect the body

astronomy the scientific study of stars, planets and other objects in space

Blitz the name given to the German bombing raids on Britain during World War Two

caravel a small, fast sailing ship of the 15th to 17th centuries

century one hundred years

conquer to defeat, usually in a war or a battle

craftsperson a person who is skilled at a craft, such as jewellery-making, furniture-making or metalwork

development the process of growing or progressing

discover to find or see something for the first time

docks an area in a port where ships are loaded and unloaded

empire an area, usually comprising many countries, ruled by an emperor or empress

engineering the use of science, technology and maths to work out the best way to create new things or to improve a product

event something important that happens

exotic unusual and exciting, coming from distant lands

explorer someone who goes on a journey to learn about new people and places

export to sell goods to other countries

family tree a diagram that shows how people in a family are related to each other

fertile soil or land that is very good for growing crops or other plants

festival a day or period of celebration

fire-break a gap in the path of a fire that acts as a barrier to slow or stop a fire spreading

flat an apartment, sometimes contained within a high-rise building

founded established or begun

goods things that people trade, for example food, tools, clothing and luxury items

government the group of people who make the laws in a country

grammar school a school for richer children, where the students learned Latin grammar and other subjects

hornbook a wooden board with the alphabet and prayers written on it, used by schoolchildren

housing estate a group of houses and other buildings built together as a single development

import to buy goods from other countries

indigo a dark blue dye obtained from plants

Industrial Revolution a period of change that saw the replacement of hand tools with power-driven machines, the building of factories and the mass movement of people from the countryside into the towns and cities. It began in Britain in the 1760s CE and happened in many other countries soon after.

inherit to receive money, property or a title after the death of the previous owner

invade to enter, using force

invention a new process or object that did not previously exist

jousting sporting combat between two knights on horseback – each knight holds a blunt lance and tries to knock the other knight from his horse

knarr boat a Viking merchant boat

labourer a person who carries out unskilled manual work

linen a cloth woven from fibres of the flax plant

longboat a long, narrow boat used by Viking explorers and warriors

manuscript a book or document that is written by hand

merchant someone who buys and sells goods

Middle Ages the period of European history from the fall of the Roman Empire in the West (5th century CE) to the fall of Constantinople (1453 CE)

mint a place where money is made

monarch a king, queen or emperor

monument a building or object that reminds people of a person or event

museum a building where historical or other interesting objects are displayed

natives local inhabitants

navigator a person who explores at sea

observatory a building used for making observations of the stars and planets

outlaw to ban from a town or village forever

plague a deadly disease that killed many people

port a town with a harbour and equipment for loading and unloading ships

portrait a painting or photo of a person

pottery items made from clay and baked to become hard

preserve to treat in a way to prevent rotting

printing the process of creating books or newspapers using moveable letter plates

quill pen a feather, dipped in ink, that was used to write with

raid a surprise attack to steal objects, animals or people or to destroy property; to attack quickly and unexpectedly to steal or to destroy property

rebuild to build something again after it has been damaged or destroyed

record to write about events so people will know about them in the future

reign the period of time when one king or queen rules

Renaissance a period of new learning, discovery and exploration in European history, from the 1400s to the 1600s CE

saga a long story about exciting adventures and brave heroes

sailor a person who works on a boat or ship

scholar a person who is highly educated

scientist a person who studies the natural world by making observations and doing experiments

sculptor an artist who produces artwork by shaping materials such as stone or clay

scurvy a disease caused by a lack of vitamin C

settle to stay and live in a place

settlement a place where people live and make a community

sewers channels for carrying away drainage water and waste water

shelter a place that provides protection from bad weather or danger

Glossary

social class a group of people who all have similar levels of wealth, influence and status

society all the people living in a country, with shared traditions, laws, interests and activities

symbol an object that represents something else

tar a thick, black, sticky substance made from wood or coal

tax money collected by a ruler or government

technology a scientific invention or industrial process; the use of science to invent new things or to solve problems

thatched covered with straw or rushes to make a roof

the past all the time before now

theatre a building for performing plays, with seats for the audience

Thing a large open-air meeting where the Vikings discussed local issues and voted for new laws

timeline a way of showing events in order of when they happened, along a line

tourism travelling for pleasure

tournament a sporting competition with several stages and one winner

trade buying and selling goods

trade route a long network of roads or sea routes that merchants and traders used to transport goods between one place and another

tribe a group of families and relatives who have the same language, customs and beliefs

Tudor the period in English history between 1485 CE and 1603 CE

turf a layer of grass and soil held together by grass and plant roots

voyage a long journey

warrior a soldier

watch a group of sailors who worked together on board a ship